THE CONTEMPLATIVE LODGE

A MANUAL FOR MASONS DOING INNER WORK TOGETHER

C.R. DUNNING, JR.

The Contemplative Lodge:
A Manual for Masons Doing Inner Work Together

Published By:

Stone Guild Publishing
P.O. Box 250167
Plano, TX 75025-0167
http://www.stoneguildpublishing.com/

First Paperback Edition Published 2021

ISBN-13 978-1-60532-076-2
ISBN- 1-60532-076-5

10 9 8 7 6 5 4 3 2 1

.

THIS WORK IS DEDICATED TO
DIVINE WISDOM

"Wisdom dwells with contemplation; there we must seek her."

"Does not wisdom call, and does not understanding raise her voice?"

"I, wisdom, dwell in prudence, and I find knowledge and discretion. I love those who love me, and those who seek me diligently find me."

"The Lord created me at the beginning of His work, the first of His acts of long ago. When He established the heavens, I was there, when He drew a circle on the face of the deep, when He marked out the foundations of the earth, then I was beside Him, like a master worker; and I was daily His delight, rejoicing before Him always, rejoicing in His inhabited world and delighting in the human race."

"And now, my children, listen to me: happy are those who keep my ways. Hear instruction and be wise, and do not neglect it."

— Redacted from Proverbs 8

ACKNOWLEDGMENTS

- Erik Arneson, for editing the manuscript and enthusiastically advocating contemplative practice in Masonry

- Kevin and Lisa Main of Stone Guild, for their hard work in producing this book

- The many individual Masons, podcasts, electronic and print publications, and the lodges and other Masonic organizations who have supported my work and prompted a book specifically addressing group contemplative practice

- T∴F∴S∴, for cherished companionship, wise counsel, and profound inspiration

- The Grand Lodge of North Carolina's Middle Chamber education program, headed by Ben Wallace, for including my work in their groundbreaking curriculum of esoteric studies

- Susan Dunning, for loving partnership with indispensable support and encouragement

Finally, I give special acknowledgement to the late Dr. Jim Tresner, 33° Grand Cross (November 11, 1941 – July 12, 2018). He was a phenomenal scholar of Masonry and many other subjects, a philosopher, a contemplative, and a profoundly loving soul. Jim was also a beloved mentor to many men, including me. My work in Masonry owes a great deal to his writing, leadership, and friendship. Jim exemplified these words from Albert Pike: "What we do for others and the world remains and is immortal."

TABLE OF CONTENTS

ILLUSTRATIONS

Front Cover: Flynn, Ryan, *The Contemplative Lodge*, 2019.

Inside Cover: Artist unknown, Beehive. Cross, Jeremy L., *True Masonic Chart*, 1857, from *http://freemasonry.bcy.ca/graphics. html*, accessed 2019.

Dedication: Dunning Jr., C.R., *Divine Wisdom, Queen of Masonry*, composite of public domain images, 2019.

Page 23: Artist unknown, *Columns and Checkerboard*, Cascade Lodge No. 12, 1925, from *http://freemasonry.bcy.ca/graphics. html*, accessed 2019.

Page 45: Artist unknown, *Solomon Building the Temple at Jerusalem*, Raphael Bible, 1615, from *https://www.britishmuseum. org/research/collection_online/collection_object_details/collection_ image_gallery.aspx?assetId=69125001&objectId=1445405& partId=1*, accessed 2019.

Page 81: Artist unknown, *Quator Coronati*, from *http://www. freemasonry.bcy.ca/aqc/aqc.gif*, accessed 2019.

Page 85: Dunning Jr., C.R., *Trestle Board of Masonic Contemplative Leadership*, 2019.

Page 101: Artist unknown, *ClipartLook*, Masonic Clipart, from *http://clipartlook.com/img-72945.html*, accessed 2019.

Page 109: Artist unknown, *Working Tools*, Grand Lodge of British Columbia & Yukon, c. 1950, from *http://freemasonry. bcy.ca/graphics.html*, accessed 2019.

FOREWORD
BY ROBERT G. DAVIS, 33° G.C.

The rituals of Freemasonry are filled with references to temple building. The English word "temple" derives from the Latin word *templum*, which anciently meant the *celestial abode of the gods*, a consecrated place where divine communication may occur. In Masonry, we normally think of a temple in the context of King Solomon's Temple. But in a deeper sense, *templum* refers not only to a place, but also to the activity of marking off and constructing such a place. Temple building is a process whereby God and humanity can encounter each other. In fact, the lessons of Freemasonry are all centered around this metaphor of building an improved version of ourselves as a temple to God, cultivating our understanding in the most sacred source of our being – *that spiritual edifice within*.

We learn in the first degree of Freemasonry that our first craving is for light – that divine and intellectual light which emanates from the primal source of all things. Our quest, then, is for nothing less than the light of the soul. We are instructed that Deity can be found residing in our own personal temples, provided we have adequately prepared. To accomplish this purpose, we take the work of Solomon's Temple as an allegory for the construction of our own spiritual temples.

But how do we go about performing this task? What tools do we have to facilitate this kind of relationship with the divine? In the pages of this insightful book, which Brother Dunning refers to as a *manual for doing the work of the lodge together*, he answers these questions for us. From his extensive career as a mental health professional and educator, he well understands the processes of psychosocial development in men. He is also an esoteric Freemason who is widely regarded in the areas of Masonic meditation practices, symbolic interpretations of Masonic ritual, and exploring the internal images of Freemasonry through its own social, psychological, and spiritual structure. Brother Dunning thus has a remarkably refined understanding of the processes of contemplative building.

In this substantive continuation and expansion of the applications of mindfulness and meditation presented in his first book, *Contemplative Masonry*, Dunning builds on the group dynamics of contemplative practices. Based upon his experience in applying meditative techniques across several disciplines, he offers the perspective that there are many benefits of communal contemplative practice that can enhance our work as Freemasons. He shows how to engage the lodge in contemplative dialogue, using the language of our rituals to compel interest and interaction among members. He gives the advocate an array of approaches that can encourage members to welcome and value contemplative practices, even when they may not consider themselves to be esoteric Masons. He teaches us the qualities of contemplative leadership and how they can be applied. Thus, we may learn to build our personal temples together in shared effort and mutual support.

No one can read this book without having a vastly enlightened understanding of how possessing a contemplative spirit enables each brother in lodge to function more fully and properly as a Master Mason. Brother Dunning convincingly affirms that, as initiated men, we are contemplative by nature. Our spiritual temple is our venue for contemplation. Only when we listen to Deity in the quiet of our innermost selves do we learn how to access divine instructions for approaching perfection. We are, therefore, naturally induced to practice contemplation, and the practice of it leads us to greater fulfillment of our potentials as social, moral, and spiritual beings.

The Contemplative Lodge provides the reader a conducive classroom for God's instruction. To be a man-temple is to be a place of contemplation, a consecrated center for uncovering the ultimate reality that is the God within us. My brethren, may we all take on our sacred responsibility of building the temple of our lives. Let me assure you that Brother Dunning is a great teacher and mentor in this kind of *Templum*.

PREFACE

Dear Reader,

Thank you for opening this book. Before you go further, I hope you will bear with me for a moment as I address you a little more personally. It is my experience that sustained, sincere contemplative practice changes us internally, and when things actually do change in our hearts and minds, then the decisions we make, the actions we take, and our relationships with others naturally reflect those changes. Borrowing from Orville Dewey, Albert Pike writes: "We are to hear and read and meditate, that we may *act* well; and the *action* of Life is itself the great field for spiritual improvement."[1] So I genuinely want my writing and speaking to help people make real differences not only in their lives but also in the lives of others. One way I respond to that desire is by committing a portion of my royalties from this book to Masonic philanthropies. By purchasing a copy for yourself, someone else, or a library, you not only support my advocacy for

1. Pike, Albert, de Hoyos, Arturo, & Hutchens, Rex R., *Albert Pike's Morals & Dogma of the Ancient & Accepted Scottish Rite of Freemasonry, Annotated Edition.* The Supreme Council, 33o, S.J., 2011, p. 315.

contemplative practice in Masonry, you also contribute to worthy causes that benefit members of our Fraternity and other individuals, or help preserve some of our most treasured edifices.

This volume is intended to complement my previous book, *Contemplative Masonry*.[2] Many of the concepts introduced there are referenced and further elaborated here. In the first book I show how our ritual encourages contemplative practice, and I provide exercises for individuals wanting to engage the Craft in such ways. Group work is mentioned, but little explanation is offered about its importance, and there is no real guidance about how to do it. I believe that focus on individual practice reflects Masonic ritual's message that individual Masons must take personal responsibility for the inner work of Masonry, which includes seeking more light, engaging the virtues, polishing and adorning the mind, spreading the cement of brotherly love, and seeking the Lost Word. Even so, our traditional teachings make it abundantly clear that Masons can better progress in the Builder's Art by also working together. With that observation in mind, the group activities provided in this book do not require you to have read or practiced the solitary exercises in the previous volume, but solitary work and communal work do naturally enhance each other.

The value of working in groups is something I deeply appreciate, having more than three decades of experience with observing, facilitating, and teaching group dynamics in various settings. In that

---

2. Dunning, Jr., C.R., *Contemplative Masonry: Basic Applications of Meditation, Mindfulness, and Imagery for the Craft*. Stone Guild, 2016.

time, I have had, and continue to have, the great pleasure of talking with many groups of Masons about the inner work of our Craft, and engaging with some of them in contemplative practices during fraternal meetings. In doing so, I repeatedly witness how Masons doing inner work together facilitates moments of extraordinary insight, affirmation, and inspiration about actually living Masonry both within and outside of our fraternal settings. The stronger sense of belonging and companionship shared in those groups also helps motivate individual members to be more diligent in their own personal practices, which in turn enables them to bring more to the group and their fellow members. When I assist Masonic groups beginning to explore these possibilities, participants often remark upon discovering the power and joy of their shared contemplative experiences, and they express a desire for more information about how to create them. This manual is a response to that repeated request.

The present title specifically references the idea of a *contemplative lodge*. In order to begin understanding what distinguishes such a gathering of Masons, we need to first clarify what it means to be contemplative. The *intentional practice of awareness* has become my preferred short definition for contemplation. In other words, to be contemplative is to deliberately shift consciousness in order to more completely perceive and understand things. This is a refinement of the word's most common use, which is simply to denote thinking deeply about something. It remains an admittedly broad definition, unlike the more particular meanings held in certain spiritual traditions, such as Roman Catholic and Orthodox Christian mysticism.[3] With an emphasis on intention rather than form, this breadth permits us to reference, access, and employ a very diverse array of states and activities of consciousness. By further qualifying such inner work as a practice, we acknowledge it entails skills that must be learned and repeatedly applied in order to develop and maintain competence and facility, just as with any art or craft. A contemplative lodge is thus ideally one that has established contemplation as a consistently engaged element of its culture and operations. While it may be that not every lodge member is personally invested in inner work, each nonetheless understands it is a natural, respectable, and beneficial aspect of the Craft.

For various reasons, Masons may find their best opportunities for doing communal inner work do not occur within a lodge, but in another Masonic organization or an informal study group. I encourage interested Masons everywhere to develop a venue and means of working together that are appropriate and effective for their own circumstances; everything offered in this book is intended to remain useful. In any case, Masons wanting to join together for contemplative practice should be well informed on how the regulations and customs of their particular organizations shape the possibilities for doing inner work together.

In addition to recognizing the need for more information about group work, I have observed a need for contemplative leadership.

---

3. See Johnston, William, *Mystical Theology: The Science of Love*. Orbis, 1995, p. 19.

After all, leadership is a natural and necessary part of any communal endeavor. So, with regard to contemplative practice in our Craft, we need Masons who can perform these roles:

1. inspiring **advocates** for the inclusion of contemplative practices in our personal and fraternal lives;
2. knowledgeable **consultants** guiding others on how they can suitably and effectively employ contemplative practices; and
3. skillful **facilitators** providing actual contemplative experiences such as guided meditations and reflective dialogue.

The benefits of contemplative leadership are by no means limited to those individuals and groups of Masons who wish to more intentionally do the inner work of the Builder's Art. As Masons collectively ponder the present and future conditions of our fraternity, we are actually engaged in a loosely connected group contemplation. We therefore have much to gain from the presence of individuals who are more adept at advocating, consulting, and facilitating such processes.

It is hoped that the present volume helps Masons make the most of group contemplative practice within our fraternal venues. My intention is to provide a foundation grounded in tradition, and offer encouragement, sound concepts, and pragmatic tools for building on that foundation. This text is indeed meant to be a *manual*, a workbook that Masonic contemplative groups can employ over and over again. I have written it with dreams of a significant percentage of copies becoming well-worn evidence of communal inner work being done in the Craft.

In serving contemplative practice in the Builder's Art, I am inspired by certain aspects of our tradition that many candidates and members also find desirable and compelling, ones for which we have much fervency and zeal. So, I beg contemplative Masons to join me in striving to keep our passion for contemplative interests within due bounds; we should not let it come between us and those who may rightly be just as passionate about other aspects of our fraternity. If we are doing our inner work well, we will remain mindful of the Plumb, Level, Compasses, Square, and Trowel with everyone, and of the Mystic Tie that unites us all.

Finally, I feel a duty to reaffirm that no one person or group speaks for the fraternity as a whole. My views are therefore freely offered for critical consideration and acceptance or rejection as you see fit.

Sincerely and fraternally,
Chuck Dunning

CHAPTER ONE: THE COMMUNAL DIMENSION OF CONTEMPLATION IN THE CRAFT

THE COMMUNAL DIMENSION OF CONTEMPLATION IN THE CRAFT

It can be easy to think of contemplative practice as happening primarily in the context of individual withdrawal into solitude. There are good reasons for that kind of inner work, yet it is generally unnecessary and often unwise to practice exclusively in isolation. The advantages of doing inner work in groups have therefore been sought and developed by countless traditions and systems of philosophy and spirituality, across all ages and cultures. Masonry is no exception to that rule, although our traditional systems have not provided much explicit instruction on how we can more fully engage contemplative practice together as part of our fraternal experience. In this chapter, we begin addressing those possibilities by considering the relevance of communal work to our Craft. Next, we prepare for its challenges, and finally we examine how it can benefit us both individually and collectively.

RELEVANCE TO MASONRY

Our fraternal traditions make it clear that Masons are not meant to be lone actors in this world. Our mythos is not about making contemplative hermits, but contemplative builders who are competent, conscientious, and creative individuals skilled at working together in communal efforts. Consider the symbolism of a traditional statement about why we seek Masonic advancement, which is to travel in search of a master's wages. We regard those symbolic wages as beneficial to not only our own well-being, but also to our families, our fraternal companions, and their families.

In the history of temple building from which much of our tradition is drawn, Masons typically found their work in local companies of other craftsmen. In order to be successfully employed, one needed well-developed technical knowledge and skills with physical tools, but these alone were not sufficient. Builders were also required to know how to work well with others, understanding and performing responsibilities as members of interdependent, collaborative, and well-coordinated teams. Our mythos illustrates that our shared goal of building great structures for the good of humanity and to the glory of God cannot be accomplished in any other way. The work of Masonry, whether Operative or Speculative, is always done in a context of mutual benefit at many levels: personal, familial, societal, global, and even cosmic.

These lessons about working as a group are exemplified in the customs we actually practice. Consider the process of becoming a Mason, which typically begins with a petition requiring signatures from more than one recommending member. That document must then be submitted to the lodge and, if accepted, an investigation is conducted by a committee. Eventually the lodge's Master Masons are welcomed to vote on the candidate. Only after the lodge's collective assent can the individual be made a Mason, and the act of making that Mason can only be performed within a lodge with at least the minimum number of qualified members participating in the ritual. In that ritual, candidates allow themselves to be led, taught, and cared for by the members, who ideally have studied and practiced it together in order to perform as an effective unit, thus ensuring the best possible experience for all. After the ritual, the new Entered Apprentice, Fellowcraft, or Master Mason may be required to learn a catechism with the assistance of at least one other member before proving proficiency before a larger group.

Within our rituals, there are many statements and actions that underscore the importance of working together as Masons. In most jurisdictions, the first scripture read to a candidate for the Entered Apprentice degree is Psalm 133, which compares the benefits of togetherness with the blessing of eternal life.

> *Behold, how good and how pleasant it is for brethren to dwell together in unity: It is like the precious ointment upon the head that ran down upon the beard, even Aaron's beard; that went down to the skirts of his garments: As the dew of Hermon, and as the dew that descended upon the mountains of Zion: for there the Lord commanded the blessing, even life forevermore.*[4]

This essential Masonic theme is continued in the explanation of perfecting the ashlar, by which we are urged to make ourselves more fitting for *union with others* in the Celestial Temple. Each of the Principal Tenets of truth, relief, and brotherly love is likewise

---

4. Atwood, Henry C., *The Master Workman; or, True Masonic Guide.* Simons & Macoy, 1850, p. 25.

explained in such a way as to affirm its value to our relationships. The lesson of the northeast corner further highlights an act of relief as a charitable expression of brotherly love. At every turn of our fraternal lives, we see that individuals must relate well with each other in order for Masonry to be perpetuated, taught, and practiced.

Our foundational documents, rituals, and monitors provide a plethora of explicit instructions on why and how we should work together. Review the following examples from a popular Masonic guidebook of the 19th century.

From the Entered Apprentice Degree:

At your leisure hours, that you may improve in Masonic knowledge, you are to converse with well-informed brethren, who will be always as ready to give, as you will be to receive, instruction.[5]

From the Fellowcraft Degree:

By [hearing] we are enabled to enjoy the pleasures of society, and reciprocally to communicate to each other our thoughts and intentions, our purposes and desires; and thus our reason is rendered capable of exerting its utmost power and energy.

The wise and beneficent Author of Nature intended, by the formation of this sense, that we should be social creatures, and receive the greatest and most important part of our knowledge from social intercourse with each other.[6]

5. Atwood, p. 37.
6. Ibid, p. 52.

From the Master Mason Degree:

[The Trowel] is an instrument made use of by operative Masons to spread the cement which unites the building into one common mass; but we, as Free and Accepted Masons, are taught to make use of it for the more noble and glorious purpose of spreading the cement of Brotherly Love and affection; that cement which unites us into one sacred band, or society of friends and brothers, among whom no contention should ever exist, but that noble contention, or rather emulation, of who best can work and best agree.[7]

[...]

It might have pleased the great Creator of heaven and earth to have made man independent of all other beings; but as dependence is one of the strongest bonds of society, mankind were made dependent on each other for protection and security, as they thereby enjoy better opportunities of fulfilling the duties of reciprocal love and friendship. Thus was man formed for social and active life – the noblest part of the work of God; and he that will so demean himself as not to be endeavoring to add to the common stock of knowledge and understanding, may be deemed a drone in the hive of Nature, a useless member of society, and unworthy of our protection as Masons.[8]

Masonic scholars of previous generations have poignantly highlighted the value of togetherness in our contemplative Craft.

7. Ibid, p. 67.
8. Ibid, pp. 71-72.

Union and harmony constitute the essence of Freemasonry: while we enlist under that banner, the society must flourish, and privet [sic] animosities give place to peace and good fellowship. Uniting in one design, let it be our aim to be happy ourselves, and contribute to the happiness of others.[9]

Further, [the lodge] is said to be opened on, and not in, a certain Degree, which latter expression is often incorrectly used, in reference rather to the speculative than to the legal character of the meeting, to indicate, not that the members are to be circumscribed in the limits of a particular Degree, but that they are met together to unite in contemplation on the symbolic teachings and divine lessons of that Degree.[10]

How far and to what degree any of us is able to open his personal Lodge [within one's own psyche] determines our real position in Masonry.... Progress in this, as in other things, comes only with intelligent practice and sustained sincere effort. But what is quite overlooked and desirable to emphasize is the power, as an initiatory force, of an assemblage of individuals each sufficiently progressed and competent to "open his Lodge" in the sense described. Such an assembly, gathered in one place and acting with a common and definite purpose, creates as it were a vortex in the mental and psychical atmosphere....[11]

In the present day, no author has more pointedly addressed the importance of group work in Masonry than Kirk MacNulty:

9. Preston, William, *Illustrations of Masonry*. 1772. Photographic Reproduction of the 1867 Edition, Cornerstone, 2016, p. 18.
10. Mackey, Albert G., *Encyclopedia of Freemasonry*, vol. 2, New Edition, Revised and Enlarged, 1946 Masonic History Company, 1956, p. 737.
11. Wilmshurst, W.L., *The Meaning of Masonry*. 1922. Barnes and Noble edition, 1999, pp. 112-113.

This balanced combination of action, contemplation and devotion appears to have been the original concept of formal Masonic labor, and any Lodge or Masonic study group which undertakes such a curriculum seriously will find itself amply rewarded.[12]

With these elements of Masonic lore, custom, ritual, and scholarship, we can see our tradition's insistence on the mutual benefit of communal involvement for the purposes of improving ourselves and society. It should also be clear that to maximize the potentials of mutual benefit, such participation requires more than just learning and performing ritual. It entails a concerted effort to acquire and share useful knowledge and profound insight about the art and the labor of becoming wiser, stronger, and more beautiful souls – more virtuous human beings. Thus, the relationships we build in our fraternal experiences are meant to empower us to build healthier and more harmonious relationships in all parts of our lives, and thereby directly contribute to a healthier and more harmonious world. That vision for the Masonic life is a very high calling, in which one is bound to face many great challenges, which is all the more reason we may be grateful for the opportunity to join in mutual support with others intent upon answering the call.

CHALLENGES AND BENEFITS

Answering Masonry's call can be demanding on many levels – physically, psychologically, socially, and spiritually – and so it includes individual and collective efforts. It is therefore fitting that

12. MacNulty, W. Kirk, *The Way of the Craftsman: A Search for the Spiritual Essence of Craft Freemasonry*, Deluxe Edition. Plumbstone, 2017, p. 213.

the inner work of contemplative practice can be pursued in solitary *and* communal forms, each of which has its own strengths and limitations. Furthermore, each of us may be more naturally drawn to one versus the other in accord with our own particular strengths and limitations. The present aim is thus not to argue that one approach is better or more important than the other. Rather, both are important and many, if not most, people will find each assists in maximizing the benefits of the other. Given that premise, we now focus on the challenges and benefits of group contemplative work in Masonic contexts.

CHALLENGES

The common challenges of communal contemplative practice in Masonry may be considered in these interrelated categories: legal, administrative, political, and psychosocial. Masons wishing to organize group inner work should give due attention to each category, while those wishing to join already established groups may be more concerned with the last. In any case, it is wise for people engaged in communal work to prepare themselves for the kinds of difficulties they may encounter, understanding that problems can manifest in more specific ways for different individuals and groups. Finally, it should be kept in mind that challenges are not always detrimental and can instead be opportunities to learn and grow.

LEGAL

Depending upon the particular jurisdiction, the official rules of a Grand Lodge, lodge, or appendant body can have significance in working out the administrative and political issues of group

practice. Those rules can also be subject to the enforceable interpretations of various authorities, whether individuals or committees. Such
authorities may additionally be empowered to issue their own orders
in matters not explicitly covered by official documents. Organizers of
contemplative activities should therefore maintain familiarity with
the relevant matters of Masonic law, consult with the proper authorities, and govern themselves accordingly. Organizers should also consider the possible merits of acquiring documented official endorse-
ments of their aims and objectives.

POLITICAL

Under this heading, we refer to the often-sensitive matters of
maintaining peace and harmony among various individual and organizational entities within the fraternity. Careful attention to legalities
goes a long way in preventing many potential political conflicts, but
may not be sufficient to prevent them all, let alone remedy those that
might arise despite an impeccable legal standing. It is therefore wise
for organizers to reach out to other persons or groups with a vested
interest in the pursuit of group contemplative practice in Masonry,
or who might otherwise regard themselves as significantly affected by
such work.

Similarly, organizers should be mindful that many Masons
have established noteworthy personal presence through years of
committed service. Such individuals may expect that their counsel
or blessings should be sought before anything new is done within their circles of influence, even if they have little to no personal
knowledge about a project's particular nature or goals. In the best
cases, Masons of such standing well deserve to be consulted, and they

can be invaluable advisors and allies. In the worst cases, they may regard any failure to consult with them as highly suspicious, even insidious, and thus feel compelled to stand in forceful opposition to the new venture.

Political issues are also powerfully shaped by the dominant cultural norms for a given locale. For example, despite Masonry's ideals of openness and tolerance, the acceptability of topics for discussion, sources of information, or types of contemplative activity can all be greatly affected by prevailing religious beliefs and attitudes. Individuals or groups perceived as crossing those often fuzzy and arbitrary boundaries can unwittingly set off conflicts that crush any possibility of progress, and which may have ramifications far beyond the immediate circumstances. Careful organizers of group contemplative work should therefore study those boundaries and frequently revisit the pros and cons of testing, crossing, or altogether avoiding them.

Within the fraternity there can also be political norms that exist independent of the dominant non-Masonic culture. Perhaps most noteworthy of such norms is a strong bias against instituting any practice perceived as uncustomary, foreign, or somehow challenging to the status quo. Related to that norm is the common human inclination to resist anything that has the potential to complicate our lives, which can certainly become a political factor when it touches on the operation of Masonic meetings or other organizational systems. So, organizers of communal inner work should be thoroughly informed about the relevance and benefits of contemplation to Masonry, and use that knowledge to help pave the way for accomplishing their aims as well as diplomatically responding to objections that might arise once the work is in practice.

A further political challenge may arise for contemplative groups who make inadequate use of the Compasses, Level, and Trowel. In other words, significant fraternal problems can arise whenever contemplative Masons display any of these attitudes and behaviors:

1. being overzealous in promoting contemplative practice;
2. acting as if contemplative practice is somehow reserved for an elite or superior class of Masons; or
3. treating Masons less interested in contemplative practice as if they are less deserving of respect, brotherly love, or affection.

It should be no surprise that groups or individuals exhibiting any of those follies draw unfavorable attention to themselves and resistance to their efforts. The organizers and participants of contemplative groups must therefore remain mindful that our Craft is rightly composed of individuals with many different interests and talents, that this diversity significantly benefits the fraternity as a whole, and that all who keep our obligations are worthy of honor, care, and kindness as fraternal equals.

ADMINISTRATIVE

The administrative challenges of contemplative group work can be so detailed and vary so much depending upon the particular environment, that we will not attempt an exhaustive examination of them. Instead, a comprehensive list of administrative matters is provided, along with questions to stimulate a thorough preparatory process. Some of these points are addressed more extensively later in this book.

- *Oversight* – Who has immediate authority over the organizers of the work? What sort of reporting is expected? If the work is being done in an informal meeting outside of the usual fraternal settings, then what if any oversight is necessary or advisable?

- *Organization* – Who handles coordination of events and duties? How will communication with potential participants occur? If activities and participation will be tracked, recorded, and assessed, how will these things be done?

- *Setting* – Where will contemplative activities occur? To what extent is a lodge room or the ritual space of another body available? What, if anything, can be done in the course of regular fraternal meetings? What about immediately before the opening or after the closing of such meetings? What atmosphere will be created and how will that be done?

- *Scheduling* – When, how often, and for how long, will the work occur?

- *Content* – How will topics and activities be determined? What topics and activities are to be avoided?

- *Facilitation* – Who will lead inner work activities such as meditation or contemplative discourse? What qualifications are expected of facilitators?

- *Supplies* – What materials and equipment will be used? Will the activities make use of Masonic working tools, furniture, incense, music, candlelight, audiovisual media, handouts, etc.? Will refreshments be provided? Who will be responsible for ensuring supplies are acquired and ready for use?

PSYCHOSOCIAL

Psychosocial refers to the dynamics and effects of interactions between individuals and their social contexts. This category of challenges therefore addresses those commonly emerging between participants in group inner work as well as within individuals' own psyches. These challenges include members being confronted with their differences, the struggle of communing versus conforming, and encountering their own internal ruffians.

We should acknowledge that the potential for interpersonal discomfort, strained relationships, and even overt conflict can arise when individuals encounter their differences in beliefs, knowledge, feelings, and behaviors about things they regard as important. Even without violating the Craft's traditional prohibition of religious and political dispute, the potential for discord can be magnified when members converse on matters of spirituality, philosophy, and morality, which are at the core of our values, decisions, and actions. Given that such matters are the focus of our Craft, and that inner work takes people even deeper into them, the organizers and participants of Masonic contemplative groups should commit to and conscientiously work toward a truly exceptional degree of mutual understanding and support.

Other psychosocial challenges are related to the difficulty of participants communing with each other as fully functioning individuals. In most groups, there is some amount of pressure to conform to the predominant ways of thinking and behaving. It can come from within a person's own psyche or from other members of the group, and it can come from both at the same time. In Masonry, this pressure can increase whenever anyone misconstrues our traditional admonition to work together in peace, harmony, and unity as a charge for homogeneity in thoughts, words, and deeds. This phenomenon tends to be detrimental because it can lead individuals to withdraw into silent compliance or, even worse, adopt the group's predominant ideas and attitudes with little or no critical process. Such capitulation to the group mind can feel comforting and even inspiring and illuminating, and the group may reward it with praise and status. Among its many problems, however, is the lack of real internal growth for the individual as an authentically whole human being. The resulting loss of the individual's potential to genuinely benefit the group with unique perspectives, insights, and questions, in turn, means less potential for a truly transformative synergy to arise within the group. With awareness of the challenges in communing versus conforming, organizers and participants in contemplative groups should encourage and support each other in meeting on the level, exercising both critical and original thinking, and welcoming the expression of divergent opinions and attitudes.

Intimately interwoven with, but certainly not limited to, all the previous psychosocial challenges are participants' confrontations with their own internal ruffians, which are their self-deceptions, ignorance, irrational fears, prejudices, vices, and the conflicts within their personal beliefs, values, and feelings. These are universal elements of the human psyche, and inner work can amplify our awareness of them. Struggling with these things can sometimes contribute to impatience, a lack of empathy and compassion, judgmentalism, and even hostility, all of which contemplatives may experience not only within themselves but also direct outward. A prescience of such difficulties can move some people to react defensively to contemplative practice, giving it less than wholehearted effort, avoiding it entirely, ridiculing it, or perhaps even actively opposing it. Masons doing inner work together are therefore wise to remember that each is striving to employ the Gavel, and that the rough and rugged road of willingly confronting their own internal ruffians is a necessary part of the journey of illumination and transformation. Furthermore, they should endeavor to embrace one another with the Five Points of Fellowship, making use of all their working tools to encourage and support themselves and each other.

Challenges as Opportunities

Preparation for the possible challenges of group inner work not only makes those challenges easier to manage, but actually prevents some of them. It also enables groups and individuals to turn challenges into moments of learning and growth, thus making them very beneficial experiences. Furthermore, many challenges may be intentionally sought precisely for their potential to enhance the natural benefits of contemplative work, a concept we will examine in the next section. Masons can make the best of even the most demanding group contemplative experience by regarding it as an actual workshop for developing and refining themselves as apprentices, craftsmen, and perhaps masters in the moral and social virtues of the Builder's Art.

BENEFITS

In *Contemplative Masonry*, three types of relationships are highlighted as central to the benefits of our Craft: membership, teaching, and initiating.[13] Membership is the aspect of our fraternal experience that bestows the benefits of *belonging*. The teaching relationship develops the benefits of *understanding*. The initiating relationship is concerned with the benefits of *transformation*, which entails being tested and advanced to new levels of awareness, competence, and responsibility. Communal inner work offers a great deal to enhance the benefits in all three areas, and not only for the participants themselves, but also extending into their fraternal environment and beyond.

BELONGING

A sense of belonging is facilitated by the good faith and familiarity that grows between members who lower their defensive barriers and encourage each other to share deeper feelings, ideas, questions, inspirations, and challenges. The process of normalization contributes to this experience of trust and connectedness, because normalization is the discovery of how much people have in common when they risk revealing what they feared were oddities. They often instead find they are not at all alone; that their particular confusions, concerns, or creative leaps are similar if not identical to those of others, and are thus more normal than previously suspected. Furthermore,

13. Dunning, Jr., C.R., *Contemplative Masonry*, pp. 56-64.

one's bond with others can be amplified simply by knowing there are shared interests and intentions among those present for group contemplation. Beyond all these well-known psychological dynamics, there may also be an interaction of subtle energies leading participants to spiritually harmonize with each other, somewhat like tuning forks resonating with a particular frequency of sound.

UNDERSTANDING

Group contemplative work can also provide much assistance in the development of knowledge and understanding. The group itself can act as a collective teacher, providing members with opportunities to consider, research, or prepare information to be shared in the group that otherwise might have remained unrecognized or underappreciated. As part of this process, various individuals may contribute different bits of information for others to analyze or integrate into their own thinking. Additionally, members can learn by observing each other actually modeling behaviors during group interactions, such as forms of contemplative practice and ways of relating to others that are aligned with the ideals of our Craft. Group contemplative exercises may also facilitate members learning more about themselves by directly observing the various functions of their psyches in meditation, and accessing memories, dreams, beliefs, hopes, fears, or other things that had been forgotten or had never before risen to conscious awareness.

TRANSFORMATION

Many of the previous benefits can contribute to an experience of transformation, which is a substantial shift in an individual's consciousness and presence in the world. However, a group engaged in inner work can also act in a more overtly initiatic manner. For example, when a member shares an idea with the group, welcoming the group's critique can result in the idea being tested for its creativity, logic, clarity, and practicality. Such feedback can be a kind of initiatic trial, a challenge not only to the idea itself but, at least implicitly, to the mind that presented it. That kind of challenge can on one hand provide powerful confirmation, or on the other hand may facilitate a timely disillusionment, in either case marking a moment of noteworthy change in one's thinking and self-concept. Another possibility for transformation can arise when individuals within a group all become focused on a particular matter. A synergy may emerge in which the members, together, generate a new insight that is greater than the sum of the parts. Such synergy can carry participants into different perspectives than they might have ever come to on their own. A radically new perspective may then act as a key factor in realigning the rest of one's life, and thus be regarded as genuinely transformative. Finally, some types of group meditative exercises, including the contemplative performance of ritual, have the potential to usher participants into spiritual experiences or states of consciousness that do indeed initiate life-changing transformations.

EXTENSION OF THE BENEFITS

Before leaving our consideration of these benefits, we should note the possibilities of their impact on broader scales. A group as a whole unit can become more empowered as its participants develop a greater mutual sense of belonging, share more knowledge and understanding with each other, and experience their own transformations while witnessing those of others. Indeed, the consistent manifestation of a transformative synergy within the group is evidence of such empowerment. Furthermore, the effects can – and our traditional teachings suggest they should – reach beyond the limits of the contemplative group itself. Through the inspired actions of its participants as they engage with other Masons, a well-functioning contemplative group effectively radiates its benefits out into the larger structures of the fraternity. These members have the potential to encourage and assist other individuals and groups to experience and express Masonry in deeper and more meaningful ways, who in turn may then be motivated to begin similar kinds of inner work for the benefit of themselves, their lodges, and other fraternal bodies. By extension, our fraternity as a whole has much to gain from the presence of healthy contemplative groups, and thereby can have a more beneficial effect on our local communities and on the world at large.

QUESTIONS FOR FURTHER CONTEMPLATION OF THE COMMUNAL DIMENSION

- To what extent have you engaged in both dimensions of Masonic inner work, both the individual and the communal?

- In what ways might it benefit you and other Masons to join in contemplative practice together?

- Within your circle of Masonic friends and acquaintances, who else might be interested in creating opportunities for Masons to do inner work together?

- With regard to your personal and local circumstances, what are the biggest challenges you foresee in pursuing communal contemplative work in Masonry?

- What talents, skills, or experiences do you have that would be valuable to addressing those challenges?

- How might you work with others to carefully and effectively address those challenges?

- Who should you consult about how to be most successful?

- What resources could help you be most successful?

CHAPTER TWO:
WAYS OF WORKING
TOGETHER

Ways of Working Together

It has been shown that contemplation not only has a rightful place in the Builder's Art, but that our tradition repeatedly encourages it. Even so, there are few explicit instructions in our rituals or monitors about the kinds of practices Masons can undertake together in order to receive as much Masonic light as possible. In responding to this deficit, it can be tempting for Masons to focus on other traditions or systems where such instruction is provided in great detail. While explorations of that nature can be worthwhile, they can also bring unnecessary complications and even outright opposition to groups of Masons wanting to pursue inner work together. This chapter offers an overview of three general types of group inner work that are wholly concerned with the symbolism, teachings, and work of our Craft: contemplative discourse, group meditation, and contemplative ritual. They are supported by appendices with step-by-step guides for activities.

Before continuing into the main body of this chapter, it is important to note that the legal, political, administrative, and psychosocial environment of a given Masonic venue may not allow for the more structured, complex, and time-consuming activities described. Even so, there may be small opportunities to introduce contemplative moments, and Masons are encouraged to seek and creatively respond to them. For example, in many jurisdictions there is a traditional moment set aside for music in the opening or closing of the lodge. That moment can be used for the playing or singing together of meditative or inspirational music, something that brings the participants together in a more focused, peaceful, and harmonious state of mind. Another opportunity arises in some ritual closings when the Master of the Lodge asks if anyone has anything to offer for the good of the Craft. A member of the lodge might then provide a focal point for a short silent meditation before the closing ritual resumes. In just about any Masonic meeting, there are moments when the presiding officer has authority to provide comments, instructions, or put Masons to work in some other way. At such times, there may be limitless possibilities, such as inviting a member to stand and share a personal understanding or application of a Masonic working tool or other symbol. In proceeding through this chapter, consider how the various ways of working together might be adapted to the Masonic venues in which you participate.

CONTEMPLATIVE DISCOURSE

Very early in our intiatic journey, we learn that Masons should, together, pursue instruction in Masonic knowledgea and that we should seek and give good counsel with each other. As shown in the previous chapter, the importance of meaningful communication among Masons is further emphasized by the lectures on hearing and the beehive. Contemplative discourse is therefore presented as fitting and vital for any group of Masons doing inner work together, and it can be combined with other kinds of practice or done entirely on its own. This section clarifies the general nature of contemplative discourse, how it differs from other forms of communication, and how it can be usefully applied in Masonic settings.

WHAT IT IS AND WHAT IT IS NOT

Contemplative discourse can be simply described as a process of exploratory communication among two or more people. Its primary aim is to increase the breadth and depth of understanding about a shared topic of consideration. Contemplative discourse is also an egalitarian process in which nobody is identified as the sole source of information. Instead, participants meet as collaborative partners, committed to seeking and valuing each other's contributions to the conversation. Participants assist each other by offering their own thoughts and feelings, while also opening their hearts and minds to different perspectives within the group. In doing so, members give careful attention to their own internal processes as well as to the ideas communicated by others. Moments of silence can therefore be frequent in contemplative discourse. Questions are a significant element of such conversations, including broad inquiries offered to the group as a whole, as well as more specific questions directed at individuals in order to encourage their input or facilitate understanding of things they have shared.

Dialogues of this nature differ significantly from other forms of communication, such as lectures, reaching agreements, or solving problems. Contemplative discourse works best when participants understand that agreement is not necessary in order to benefit from their time together. In fact, pressure to reach agreement can actually stifle the process of offering and considering different perspectives and possibilities. A problem-solving mindset can similarly interfere with such aims. While the critical thinking employed in problem-solving is also important in contemplative discourse, the goal is not to chip away possibilities of meaning until the group arrives at a single truth to be accepted by everyone. Furthermore, problem-solving approaches are sometimes limited by their focus on intellect and their lack of attention to other dimensions of the soul. By contrast, participants in contemplative discourse demonstrate care for each other as whole human beings. They conduct themselves with understanding that people's beliefs, values, and sense of meaning and purpose are all inextricably interconnected with their feelings, intuitions, hopes, and dreams, not only their rational thought processes. They know that their most powerful questions, insights, and inspirations often mysteriously emerge from the deepest parts of their being, rather than following from strictly logical processes like mathematical formulae.

APPLICATION IN THE CRAFT

The practice of contemplative discourse in Masonry offers participants the opportunity to join in reverent, mutually supportive exploration of the symbols, teachings, and experiences of our Craft.

This section reviews and explains the most significant elements of a typical session of contemplative discourse.[14]

It is a Masonic custom to invoke the aid of Deity before beginning our labors. Masons therefore fittingly start sessions of contemplative discourse with a moment of silence in which participants may inwardly seek spiritual assistance in their own ways. It is important that these moments are not rushed, and not only to give adequate time for prayer, but also to facilitate the natural process of relaxing the body and quieting the mind that begins when people become still. Ending sessions with a moment of silence is also a good idea in that it provides participants an opportunity to collect their thoughts and offer thanks to Deity if they feel so inclined.

Once a suitable period of silence has been observed at the opening, the facilitator asks participants to focus their hearts and minds on a single word, short phrase, and/or image offered as a common focal point for the group. This focal point can be one previously announced, or it can be one chosen in the moment by the group, by the facilitator, or totally at random such as in drawing one from a number of possibilities. If the focal point is an object, having an example physically present can also be helpful.

With the group focused on the topic, participants are welcomed to contribute their insights, feelings, and questions to begin the process of exploring its possible meanings. That process always involves at least one of two types of thinking – reflection and

14. Appendix B provides example scripts.

speculation – both of which are intimately interwoven with our common fraternal experiences. Indeed, for more than three centuries, our Craft has qualified itself as a speculative art, and the content of our degree catechisms is a formalized procedure of reflection and speculation on our initiatic experiences. In contemplative discourse, participants more freely engage these two kinds of thinking by either implicitly or explicitly addressing questions such as these:

- What seems superficially obvious about the focal point, without any traditional or ritual explanations? How might these simple observations have symbolic or allegorical meaning?

- What were the contexts – time, place, and other circumstances – in which participants each first experienced the focal point, and how might the contexts affect the meaning?

- What thoughts, feelings, or questions first arose for participants during the initial moments of their original experience of the focal point? What meanings might they suggest?

- How is the focal point identical or similar to other things, whether inside or outside Masonry, and how might the meanings of those things be relevant?

- If participants open their hearts and minds to the widest range of possibilities, without any concern for being correct or making sense, what hunches, intuitions, inspirations, or questions arise?

- How might multiple meanings, or layers of meaning, be simultaneously present for the focal point, even if they seem to contradict each other?

To maximize the benefits of contemplative discourse, it is important that participants understand and respect the difference between traditional meanings and personal meanings for our symbols and teachings. Traditional meanings are those specified in our rituals and monitors, or those from other sources that are widely agreed upon within the fraternity and have stood the test of time. Personal meanings result from an individual's own studies, contemplations, and other experiences. They may significantly diverge from traditional meanings. Beyond comprehending these differences, it is crucial in contemplative discourse to regard both kinds of meaning as valid within their own contexts. Contemplative discourse should proceed with an affirmation that no individual or organization within the Craft has the right to demand that Masons limit their personal understandings to the traditional meanings, just as individuals should not expect their personal meanings be approved or adopted by others. This affirmation helps avoid pressures to conform and ensures a more open sharing of thoughts and feelings, which in turn increases the potential for everyone to experience more belonging, increase knowledge and understanding, and encounter transformation.

There are two more elements vital to contemplative discourse, especially with regard to producing truly useful insights. While an openness to different perspectives and understandings is vital to contemplative discourse, so is the effort to carefully examine things and clarify our thinking about them. It is wise for participants to welcome evaluation of the evidence and logic of their ideas, rather than discovering it in less constructive and supportive circumstances. Similarly, participants should ask themselves and each other about the practicality of their insights, or how they might actually be useful for improving one's life or the lives of others, whether internally or externally. In fact, it is good practice for participants to wrap up their conversation by discussing upcoming opportunities to apply their insights. These two aims of clarity and practicality in contemplative discourse can help it avoid becoming confusing and vain, and they can also help prevent it being regarded by others as worthless or even detrimental to the Craft.

GROUP MEDITATION

As with contemplation, the term *meditation* can have different specific meanings from one tradition, system, or authority to another. For the present purposes, we are speaking of fairly formalized methods of contemplative practice that typically, but not exclusively, involve sitting still and closing the eyes, and then using a particular process to directly shift consciousness toward desired states and purposes. Meditation has an endless number of forms and applications, many of which can be combined. Before delving into types of communal meditation that can benefit Masonic inner work, we must first dispel some troublesome myths about meditation.

MYTHS ABOUT MEDITATION

It is a myth that the overarching goal of every meditation is to empty the mind of all thoughts. While it is desirable for the mind to become calmer and quieter, especially in silent sitting, it can actually be quite counterproductive to expect that this calmness will happen in some extraordinary way, especially to the extreme of having no thoughts whatsoever. In fact, due to this myth, many people quickly abandon the practice of meditation, convinced their inability to "turn off" their thoughts is a failure that proves there is no hope of ever accomplishing their mistaken goal. Based on misconceptions and experiences like these, some people even wrongly judge themselves as somehow psychologically unfit for the practice of meditation. The truth is that the inner voice, mental images, and sense perceptions can intrude upon even seasoned meditators who are familiar with significant states of inner quietude. Practitioners should acknowledge any such expectations in themselves and begin replacing them with the understanding that there are benefits to gain from the experience of meditation however it actually happens. If nothing else, one should understand that the skills of meditation are like those of any other activity in that improvement comes with patient practice.

A closely related myth is that meditating means attaining and maintaining unbroken focus, never becoming distracted, perhaps not even noticing anything else going on within or around oneself. As with the previous myth, this one contains an unrealistic all-or-nothing assumption, misconstrues desirable conditions as the necessary goal, and judges anything less than the idealized perfection as failure. It likewise does far more to discourage the practice of meditation than motivate people to benefit from the experience. Practitioners should learn to embrace the process of recognizing distraction and redirecting attention toward its intended focus as a positive and beneficial part of their inner work.

Finally, it is necessary to address the notion that if meditation is properly performed, then one should experience something fantastic, like profound mystical ecstasy, dramatic visitation by spiritual beings, transportation of consciousness out of the body and even into other worlds, or the development of paranormal powers. It is true that there are practices intended to lead to such experiences. It is also true that many people have claimed, perhaps some of them credibly so, to gain such benefits as a result of their inner work. Without entering into an argument about these possibilities, we instead refute the myth that experiences like these are universal goals or measures of success for the general practice of meditation. It is also worth considering that such aims and practices are not likely to be well received or tolerated for groups operating within most of our fraternal venues, and for sound reasons. Indeed, a number of contemplative traditions teach that the pursuit of such things can distract from more important forms of inner work. The point, however, is not necessarily to discourage individuals from exploring these possibilities if they so wish, but rather to keep the focus on what is fitting for Masons doing inner work together in their more or less ordinary fraternal settings.

Forms for the Craft

This section examines several kinds of group meditation with relevance to Masons doing inner work together: silent sitting, discursive meditation, chanting, guided imagery, and energy work.[15]

Silent Sitting

In a previous section, we considered the benefits of beginning and ending a session of contemplative discourse with a period of silence. Silent sitting is, however, a most worthwhile practice in its own right. It is actually the starting place for contemplative training in many traditions and systems. Despite its seemingly basic and simple nature, it can also be among the most challenging and beneficial of practices and is thus often the mainstay of inner work for experienced meditators. In passing, we note the phases presented for silent sitting are also largely used for other forms of group meditation.

The process of silent sitting recommended for most Masonic groups begins with participants sitting in chairs and settling into positions they can maintain with little to no movement for the appointed period of time. Eyes should be closed, but individuals may instead choose to direct their eyes toward something in front of them, perhaps on the floor. With this option, it helps to relax the eyes and let them go out of focus as attention turns inward. The spine should be as naturally straight as possible. Legs and ankles should not be crossed, and the soles of the feet should be on the floor. Depending on the circumstances and individual preferences, shoes may or may not be worn. The lower legs should be perpendicular to the

15. Appendix C offers example scripts for meditations in each category.

floor or at an angle sufficient to reduce pressure between the thighs and seat of the chair. Some people prefer to sit near the edge of the seat for this reason, but for others that can be too stressful on the back. Hands may be held in any position that is easy to maintain and not distracting for the participant, and some may wish to use specific hand positions from different meditative traditions. Once a good meditative posture has become habitual, simply settling into it can facilitate a significant shift into a calmer and more centered state of consciousness.

After members have settled into their positions, the group enters a phase of intentional relaxation and centering. With experienced meditators, this entire phase may require little or no prompting at all, but it is typically helpful for a facilitator to guide participants through it, especially if there are novices in the group. There are many ways to proceed, but in general a facilitator verbally assists participants in releasing unnecessary tension from the body and oxygenating the blood. Observing and perhaps silently counting breaths is a common element. In addition to aiding relaxation, these steps help participants begin to center themselves by placing their intention and attention in the present moment, listening carefully to the facilitator and becoming more aware of the things happening within them. This phase should proceed at a gentle pace and be given enough time for everyone to experience shifting into a genuinely more relaxed and centered state.

If a facilitator has been providing guidance, then the next step is to prompt the group to let go of the relaxing and centering process and simply sit with as much stillness and quietness as possible.

The facilitator may remind participants that if they find themselves becoming distracted by too many thoughts or sense perceptions, to calmly and gently return their attention to their breath as a means of re-centering. Once these instructions are given, the facilitator typically remains silent and allows participants to have their own experiences of sitting still, being outwardly quiet and nonjudgmentally aware of what is happening within.

There are many ways this practice can benefit wellness in all dimensions of their being – physical, emotional, mental, and spiritual. It is not only optimal for experiencing a greater degree of inner peace, it increases awareness of the content and operations of the psyche. Over time, it can also lead to greater awareness, acceptance, and patience with oneself, and thus tends to foment the same in one's attitudes toward others.

The final phase of silent sitting meditation often retraces some or all of the steps of centering and oxygenating the blood. Then participants are led to turn their attention back toward the environment around them, grounding themselves in their sense perceptions. To end the meditation, they are prompted to open their eyes and move more freely. Group members might then be invited to enter a period of contemplative discourse to reflect on their experiences.

Discursive Meditation

Discursive meditation is the practice of having discourse within oneself. As a formalized group meditation, participants move through the usual phases of relaxation and centering, and then the facilitator prompts them to turn their minds upon a focal point. Participants inwardly concentrate on the focal point, carefully attending to the different parts of the psyche responding to it, silently observing different perspectives and possibilities emerging within themselves. In discursive group meditation, this process is the primary intention and therefore takes the majority of the group's time, and may be followed by a period of open discourse among participants.

There are several ways of thinking about this kind of meditation that can be helpful to participants. For instance, they can ask themselves reflective and speculative questions like those provided in the earlier section on contemplative discourse. Even more depth and detail can be facilitated by understanding four different ways of working with the mind to form interpretations or discover meaning: association, analysis, intuition, and interactive imagery.[16] The group may have the facilitator briefly remind them of these various ways of contemplation at the beginning or occasionally throughout the meditation, or even guide them from one to another in turn, punctuated by periods of silence.

ASSOCIATIVE CONTEMPLATION

In associative contemplation, the aim is to discover connections between the focal point and other ideas, memories, or feelings. Some associations may be very obvious, as in those where there is great similarity between the focal point and something else, or in cases where the focal point is commonly encountered with something else. Other associations can be much less obvious, like those in which there is some small quality of the focal point shared by

---

16. These four forms of contemplation are first addressed in *Contemplative Masonry*, pp. 121-135.

something else. In any case, the meditator ponders how different associations suggest different possibilities of meaning.

ANALYTICAL CONTEMPLATION

Analytical contemplation carefully observes the focal point and attempts to break it down into different parts or qualities, each of which is examined on its own. The focal point is then considered as an assembly of all these parts relating with each other in certain ways, each logically contributing to the meaning of the whole. For a simple example, consider the two main parts of the Common Gavel, which are its handle and head. The handle's primary purpose is for gripping in order to move the head, and the head's purpose is for striking. The Gavel is thus understood as an instrument for transferring the energy of movement into the object that is struck, and thereby generating an effect upon or within that object. In this kind of contemplation, the meditator may also come to understand how the focal point is greater than the sum of its parts.

INTUITIVE CONTEMPLATION

With this type of contemplation, a meditator practices holding the focal point as the center of awareness, intentionally avoiding the processes of forming associations and analysis. The aim is to simply notice what arises from the mysterious depths of the psyche, allowing possibilities to come and go without trying to process any of them with other ways of thinking. Along the way, it may be that various possibilities bring with them stronger feelings of significance, and it can be especially tempting to devote attention to them by forming associations and performing analysis. Yet they should simply be noticed and released as attention is returned to the focal point itself, trusting that what seems most significant can later be made the focal point of another form of contemplation. After some time with this process, the meditator then removes attention from the focal point for a period of silent sitting. Possibilities may continue to emerge and be duly noted, but one's attention is redirected to sitting in silence.

INTERACTIVE CONTEMPLATION

Interactive contemplation is a process of vividly imagining oneself engaging with the focal point in some way similar to how it might be done in the material world. In this type of meditation, one invites the psyche to more or less spontaneously produce images and events that serve as means by which different possibilities can be symbolically expressed and interpreted, much as is done with dreams. As an example of the basic process, if the focal point is an object such as a working tool, the meditator could imagine actually using that tool in different ways and situations, and then ponder the symbolic possibilities. Its use might also be inwardly discussed with imaginary characters, like those appearing in Masonic legends. If the focal point is something intangible, such as a virtue or moral principle, one could imagine scenarios in which it could be employed. In some cases, it might be fitting to personify such a focal point as a character with whom one interacts. For instance, traditional anthropomorphic images of the Four Cardinal and Three Theological Virtues can be used to imagine communicating with the virtues as though they are intelligent beings capable of explaining themselves or giving instruction and advice. For communal work, a facilitator can offer particular images, characters, or settings for all participants to engage in their own unique ways.

A special consideration with this form of contemplation is that it can be quite engaging, dramatic, and even fun, but it also has risks. Meditators are therefore wise to avoid dealing with it primarily as a form of entertainment, reveling in its potentials for escapist fantasy and slipping into self-aggrandizing delusions. It should instead be respected as a powerful means of encountering, realizing, and integrating the deeper truths of the psyche and existence, and should be balanced with other forms of inner work. As with the previous forms of meditation, it can be good to follow a group session of interactive contemplation by reflecting on it in discourse among the members.

CHANTING MEDITATION

Chanting meditation, in which group members join in the repetition of a sound, word, or phrase, is practiced in many different traditions, including all the great religions. Such repetitions can be sung, spoken, whispered, or practiced silently. The purposes and effects of chant include assistance with centering and concentration, enhancing the experience of togetherness in a group, serving as a focal point for discursive meditation, amplifying particular emotions and other subtle energies, facilitating shifts into specific states of consciousness, and expressing reverence and spiritual devotion. All of these aims are fitting for Masonic contemplative groups, depending on relevant cultural factors. However, in keeping with the Craft's principle of religious inclusiveness, chanting to express reverence and spiritual devotion should be done in a way not restricted to one particular religion.[17] Therefore, chanting religiously specific names of

17. Exceptions to this rule may be appropriate in Masonic bodies with specific religious requirements.

Deity or other spiritual beings is likely to be inappropriate in most Masonic settings. On the other hand, it may well be appropriate to chant sounds or words associated with philosophical principles shared by many religions, even if they are from languages unknown to most members of the group. The chanting of words or phrases from Masonic ritual is always fitting and highly recommended. In any case, facilitators should inform participants about the sounds or words being used and the particular reasons for chanting them.

Guided Imagery

This form of meditation is like the interactive contemplation described above, except a facilitator typically provides more structure and detail while leading participants through an extended imaginary experience.[18] In effect, meditators participate in a story told by the facilitator. This type of meditation permits a more complex shared experience among group members, one that may intentionally involve a great number of symbolically represented elements and thus have much to reveal about the possible relationships and interactions between those elements and the individuals meditating upon them. It is important for the facilitator to consider the levels of experience and skill present in the group, because individuals vary on the optimal range of complexity and detail, as well as frequency and speed of transitions from one element to another. Thus, the most effective guided meditations allow enough flexibility in the imagery and space between major elements for each group member to have vivid

---

18. Guided imagery can intersect with the Art of Memory, a contemplative practice recommended for Masons as early as the Schaw Statutes of 1599. See Faulks, Martin, A Mosaic Palace – *Freemasonry and the Art of Memory*, Lewis Masonic, 2018.

and unique experiences. Participants should also be mindful that individuals naturally differ in their abilities with different kinds of imagery, such as visual images versus sounds, smells, tastes, actions, or emotions. For example, when imagining a human character, one individual may be able to clearly see the character yet be challenged by trying to converse with it, while the opposite situation may exist for someone else. With this understanding, members of the group can allow themselves to follow along in more personally productive ways, and give more attention to learning than performing.

ENERGY WORK

This heading refers to methods of working with our psycho-physiological energies, also known as *subtle energies*. Every form of meditation, and indeed every human activity, works with these energies in some way, but these methods do so more directly and powerfully, often combining special breathing techniques, chanting, imagery, and body movements. While there is a great deal of lore concerned with metaphysical possibilities of energy work, for our purposes it can be quite sufficient to regard it as a way of more powerfully finetuning our thoughts, emotions, and bodies to certain states or attitudes. Doing so as a group helps create an atmosphere conducive to particular purposes, such as aligning with, more fully integrating, and more clearly expressing specific Masonic principles.

There are various ancient traditions and systems concerned with such energies and methods, like those associated with the sefirot of the Kabbalah, the elements of psychospiritual alchemy, the planets and constellations, the chakras of yoga, or the chi meridians of Asian medicine.[19] Masonic contemplative groups may find some of these highly relevant to the Builder's Art, yet it should be noted that many methods are intimately connected with specific religious traditions and even involve the invocation of particular spiritual beings. Groups choosing to employ energy work are therefore strongly advised to carefully consider relevant cultural and political factors, engage in more universal practices, and avoid crossing the boundary between Masonry and religion.

CONTEMPLATIVE RITUAL

Whether as a candidate, a performer, or an observer, participation in Masonic ritual is a naturally contemplative experience. The entire process of preparing for and opening a meeting or ceremony is a series of exercises in establishing a proper atmosphere and attitude for each participant to become more fully aware of the ritual's multilayered symbolism in words, images, and actions. In turn, the specific form of a given meeting or ceremony makes use of numerous methods to draw attention to particular focal points, stimulating the psyche to dwell on their potential meanings in one's life. Thus, tradition supplies us with the designs of our Craft, but it is up to us to execute these processes with understanding and intentionality, thereby maximizing the benefits they offer.[20] In this section, we

19. For a comprehensive introduction to subtle energies as they are addressed in different traditions, see Lockhart, Maurine, *The Subtle Energy Body: The Complete Guide*. Inner Traditions, 2010.

20. The author also addresses this topic in "Contemplation and Ritual Initiation," an essay in French, Jedidiah and Millar, Angel, et al., *The Three Stages of Initiatic Spirituality: Craftsman, Warrior, Magician*. Lewis Masonic, 2019.

examine how groups of Masons can contemplatively engage the processes of ritual preparation, performance, and reflection.[21]

PREPARATION

Long before an official meeting, degree ritual, or installation is ever held, there is much that can be done in contemplative preparation by candidates, performers, and observers. Everyone can engage in supportive studies, and the group can instruct and join with the candidate in other contemplative practices such as mindfulness and various forms of meditation. By doing so, candidates are directly impressed with the importance of contemplative practice in the given Masonic body. Trust and cohesion is built, and everyone gains the benefits of being exposed to different perspectives on the Masonic ritual experience.

The study of appropriate reading materials provides all participants with a richer philosophical and inspirational background for the event. Some jurisdictions have official materials designed for this purpose with the degrees of initiation, and groups may also decide to develop a set of relevant Masonic and non-Masonic literature to be given to every candidate for a particular degree. Similar steps can be taken in preparing for the various offices of the body. After candidates have studied the materials, the group can meet with them for reflection in contemplative discourse.

There are many reasons contemplative discourse is an especially valuable practice in preparing for a ritual. For example, it can give

---

21. Guided meditation scripts for each phase are located in Appendix D.

candidates opportunities to reflect upon their motives, how their lives have led them to seek the given degree or office they are approaching, and how much they are willing to commit to the corresponding inner work as well as the outward duties. This not only helps them prepare for the event but helps performers and observers be more aware of its significance, especially the personal import revealed by those who will receive the ceremony. Performers and observers may also share what personally moves them to take part, which can make powerful impressions on candidates' hearts and minds.

Encouragement to practice mindfulness is another important pre-ritual function of contemplative Masonic groups.[22] Mindfulness is the intention and effort to be fully present and nonjudgmentally attentive to whatever one is actually doing. It brings meditative awareness into the immediate moment of one's actions and interactions with other people and things. By practicing mindfulness in their lives outside of ritual, members are prepared to more fully center their consciousness in the actual experience of ritual as it occurs. It can be especially helpful for performers to include mindfulness in group rehearsal of their lines and actions. Rather than focusing only on the perfection of rote recall and the too common condemnation of errors, mindful rehearsal has the potential to increase these things:

- forming habitual shifts of consciousness more likely to carry through into delivery of the ritual;

---

22. For more on the concept and practice of mindfulness in Masonry, see Dunning, *Contemplative Masonry*, pp. 95-104. Also see Kabat-Zinn, Jon. *Wherever You Go There You Are: Mindfulness in Everyday Life*. Hyperion, 1994.

- the joyful sense of participation in the flow of things and their unity and harmony with each other;

- an empathic awareness and understanding of candidates' reactions throughout a ceremony.

Group meditations can help with preparation. For example, members can meet with candidates to take the elements of petitioning, investigation, and other preliminary processes as focal points for discursive meditation and discourse. At the beginning of ritual practice sessions, as well as prior to the actual performance, silent sitting can enhance the sense of togetherness among members of the ceremonial team and observers, and help them relax, center, and clear their hearts and minds of distracting thoughts and feelings. Participants may similarly come together to engage in discursive meditation on the ceremony's central themes.[23] Groups with an interest in subtle energies can also identify which energies they wish to highlight in a ritual and then make use of meditation techniques designed to refine and amplify those energies. This work can be as broad as everyone focusing on an overarching energy associated with a particular degree or installation, or as detailed as performers practicing with more specific energies that will later be called upon for certain roles, phases, or actions within the ceremony.

---

23. While it is not a group practice per se, the Chamber of Reflection is highly recommended to prepare candidates for a more contemplative experience of the ritual. However, depending on jurisdiction, it may either be standard practice, usable at the discretion of the local body, or prohibited. For more on the Chamber of Reflection, see Hammer, Andrew, *Observing the Craft: The Pursuit of Excellence in Masonic Labour and Observance*. Mindhive, 2016, pp. 100-104. Also see Da Costa. Jr., Helio L., "The Chamber of Reflection," http://freemasonry.bcy.ca/texts/gmd1999/pondering.html, accessed 2019.

PERFORMANCE

Most jurisdictions strictly prescribe the events of ritually opening and closing their official meetings as well as the conduct of degrees and installations. While there may be points in opening and closing where the presiding offer has some discretion to permit the exercise of group meditation, this is less likely to be true during the presentation of degree or installation ceremonies. For this reason, mindfulness is the primary tool for candidates, performers, and observers to contemplatively engage with ritual during its performance. It is reiterated that mindfulness is a *nonjudgmental* awareness immersed in the present moment. This does not mean there is no attempt to shape the experience of ritual in accord with desired outcomes, for every ritual includes not only particular actions, but also thoughts and feelings that facilitate its aims. Thus, mindful participation in ritual means welcoming and accepting each passing experience as it actually happens and, rather than dwelling on it, letting it go as attention is occupied with the continuing flow of things. In addition to mindfulness, a contemplative experience of ritual can also include the use of imagery.

Mindfulness as a group practice during ritual begins with a shared understanding that the place and time of Masonic ritual is sacred. As William Preston says:

> *To begin well, is the most likely means to end well: and it is justly remarked, that when order and method are neglected at the beginning, they will be seldom found to take place at the end.*

The ceremony of opening and closing the lodge with solemnity and decorum is, therefore, universally adopted among Masons.[24]

Rather than depend solely upon the ceremony itself, everyone should take personal responsibility for ensuring an atmosphere of solemnity and decorum. Each member of the group supports the others in doing so by eliminating as many distractions as possible. Electronic devices such as phones are excluded or turned off, and all in attendance remain still and quiet except for the movement and sound required by the ritual. The group can also enhance the physical environment as sacred, extraordinary, and conducive to mindfulness through the traditional practices of low lighting, appropriate music at fitting times, and the judicious use of incense (considering possible sensitivities and/or allergies among the participants).

While establishing a favorable setting is important, it is essential that each member makes a personal commitment to the following points:

- taking responsibility for one's own attitudes;

- setting aside all other concerns by redirecting awareness to the present moment;

- taking note of one's sensory perceptions of the ritual space and events;

- focusing thoughts and actions on the immediate processes and purposes; and

- investing mindful attention in the other participants' actions and attitudes.

24. Preston, William, *Illustrations of Masonry*, p. 21.

Such a change should have already begun before entering the sacred space. Key moments to amplify it are naturally found with the donning of aprons, costumes, jewels, or other regalia, when participants can facilitate the shift by carefully recalling and resolving to think and act in accord with those items' symbolic meanings. The instant of crossing the threshold into the space itself is another important moment. One can mindfully take that step with the intention of leaving behind the profane world and the attitudes and habits of mind and body one typically has there.

Throughout ritual, it is vital to open and engage the heart, to *actually feel* the sentiments befitting our ceremonies, such as: gratitude for the opportunity to be present; respect and affection for companions; reverence for the sacredness of the moment; wonder at the mysteries behind the veils of our symbols; faith in the wisdom, strength, and beauty of our ancient tradition; hope for the most beneficial effects of the ritual; and sincere resolve to positively contribute to the experience. Such attitudes may come more spontaneously to candidates for degrees or installations, but other participants can and should intentionally stir these attitudes within themselves. For observers and performers, this work helps with being attentive and experiencing the ritual with openness to new depths of meaning. Performers further benefit by having the emotions immediately available for expression through the nuances of their voice, facial expressions, and other body movements, which in turn make the experience more significant for everyone.

Performers and observers can enhance their participation of ritual with the personal use of imagery. For example, in the Craft lodge, tradition holds there is a ray of light extending between the Three Great Lights on the altar and the Worshipful Master. The person sitting in the East can therefore benefit by imagining seeing it and feeling its warmth, and thereby open the heart and mind to more clearly sense the possibilities of inspiration and wisdom it symbolizes. Others in the lodge can also visualize that ray as a means of elevating their feelings of reverence, wonder, faith, and personal commitment to the ritual. Even specific actions can be accompanied by meaningful visualizations, such as imaging a descent of spiritual light when a candidate's hoodwink is removed. A bright stream of brotherly love flowing from the heart of an officer into the heart of the candidate can likewise be visualized at crucial moments in degree ceremonies.

As alluded in the section on contemplative preparation, meditating upon one's role, or the traditional character associated with it, also enables one to be more mindful and expressive of the specific qualities and principles that role represents during performance of ritual. In effect, one takes on a more carefully defined and crafted persona just as a serious actor would do. That kind of work can also raise countless possibilities for employing imagery as an aid to ritual, including matching certain qualities, subtle energies, or actions with particular colors. As examples, the sky's colors at dawn, dusk, and midday could be called upon as keynotes for visualizations in correspondence with the Worshipful Master, Senior Warden, and Junior Warden. This practice assists everyone to more fully recall the principles associated with the offices and the archetypal roles and mythic personalities of King Solomon, King Hiram, and Hiram Abiff.[25] In some cases, Masonic ritual actually specifies the use of color and speaks to its symbolism, as well as the attributes and attitudes of different characters. Even so, there is still much room for creative inquiry and development in this area, which could make for an ongoing group contemplative project in itself.

REFLECTION

Especially with degrees of initiation, participants can maximize the benefits of ritual by soon afterward joining in contemplative discourse for reflection. In many cases, it is customary to offer recipients a moment for reflection and comment after the final lecture and before proceeding to close. However, after having experienced so many poignant things in relatively quick succession, the recipient might fear saying something that could be judged foolish, and too often feel pressured to get things finished. It is no surprise that recipients can feel overwhelmed and have little more to express than a general impression of the ceremony and their feelings of gratitude. Much more could be accomplished with carefully structured sessions of contemplative discourse, including thoughtfully worded questions designed to facilitate the process of recalling details from the event, exploring how they affected recipients and other participants, and

---

25. This color scheme was first presented for exercises in interactive contemplation in Dunning, *Contemplative Masonry*, pp. 125-127.

considering what personal significance and applications they might have in participants' lives.

Masonic rituals provide us with a plethora of possibilities for experiential learning. Educational theorists Kolb and Fry outline this kind of learning as a process with four elements[26]:

1. an actual concrete experience;
2. observing and reflecting on the experience;
3. forming abstract concepts based on those reflections; and
4. testing the conclusions.

With regard to Masonic ritual, those elements correspond to:

1. everything participants physically do or have done to them and what they perceive via the five senses during the ritual;
2. recalling what they thought and emotionally felt in connection with those actions and perceptions;
3. speculation on meanings for the experience, in part or as a whole, which our rituals often exemplify in their lectures and scripted conversations; and
4. members putting those meanings into practice in their everyday lives, or in future performances of ritual, and the continued learning from the resulting experiences.

26. Kolb, David A. & Fry, R., "Toward an Applied Theory of Experiential Learning," in Cooper, C. (ed.), *Theories of Group Process*, John Wiley, 1975; and Kolb, David A., *Experiential Learning: Experience as the Source of Learning and Development*, Prentice-Hall, 1984.

As a communal contemplative practice, Masons can engage the second and third elements of experiential learning by taking time to meditate on the events of a recent ritual and then joining in contemplative discourse about them. For meditative recollection, it may be helpful for a facilitator to guide members through the traditional phases and events of the ritual. On the other hand, it can be beneficial to leave things less systematic, allowing different parts of the experience to spontaneously arise in the minds of meditators.

In the ensuing contemplative discourse, a good structure for the process of sharing recollections and speculating on meanings is the W^3 technique[27]. The basis of this technique is remembering and addressing three simple questions:

1. **"What?"** – This question is about the simple facts of the ritual and the most basic observations made as they were happening. Even members highly experienced in the ritual can benefit from this question, at least because it provides an easy way to start the flow of conversation.

2. **"So what?"** – Attention is given to analyzing, speculating, and conceptualizing about lessons, meanings, and uses for what was learned. Everyone is encouraged to speak of personal meanings as well as traditional meanings.

27. Lipmanowicz, Henri & McCandless, Keith, *The Surprising Power of Liberating Structures: Simple Rules to Unleash a Culture of Innovation*, Liberating Structures Press, 2014; and *Liberating Structures: Including and Unleashing Everyone*, http://www.liberatingstructures.com, accessed 2019.

3. *"Now what?"* – The focus becomes when, where, and how any conclusions will be applied and tested. The objective is to move Masonry beyond our ritual spaces, out into our attitudes and behaviors in the profane world, and into our solitary moments of contemplation and decision making.

While these questions are generally explored in sequence, it is also quite natural for some movement back and forth between them. Greater depth and detail can be prompted with additional questions related to the basic three, such as these:

WHAT?

- What were the emblems, furniture, regalia, and other things that got your attention?

- What else did you see, hear, smell, or taste?

- What roles or parts were played in the ritual?

- What were its events?

- What patterns did you observe?

- What do you recall thinking or feeling at different points along the way?

- What are your general feelings about it now?

So WHAT?

- What were the ritual's purposes, its motives, and intentions?

- What were your motives and intentions?

- Why are those motives and intentions important?

- In what ways does this experience connect with other experiences you have had or things you know?

- What seemed to be the most obvious lessons?

- What other possibilities of meaning might there be?

- What questions has this experience raised in your mind?

- How might these lessons and questions be personally relevant and useful to you?

Now what?

- What can you do to productively respond to your questions?

- How might you act on the lessons of the ritual?

- In what specific ways might you experiment with changing your thoughts and actions?

- What are some specific times and places you can enact and test these changes in the near future?

- During and after your attempts to use what you learned, who will you discuss them with?

Questions for Further Contemplation on Working Together

- With regard to the myths about meditation, to what extent has each of them been part of your attitudes about meditation?

- What is your own personal history of participating in group practices like contemplative discourse, silent sitting, the different forms of discursive meditation, chanting, guided imagery, energy work, and contemplative ritual?

- Which ones are of most interest to you, regardless of what others might think or feel about them, and why do they interest you?

- If you experience reservations within yourself about any of them, what are your concerns and how might you address them?

- Considering the legal, political, administrative, and psychosocial environments of your typical Masonic venues, how might you and others best work in order to introduce and develop group contemplative practice together?

CHAPTER THREE:
CONTEMPLATIVE LEADERSHIP

CONTEMPLATIVE LEADERSHIP

Many Masons worry about membership numbers, maintaining long established organizations, the upkeep of facilities, and continuing meaningful and visible forms of service to our communities. These things are important because they comprise a significant part of our physical presence in the world, our collective body, and its behaviors. Yet the life within a body must be nourished if the body is to be healthy and strong. Of all things necessary to human physical life, breath is the one most immediately required. In Genesis, the clay of Adam's body did not live until it received the spiritual breath of Elohim. Breath plays a similarly indispensable role in other creation stories, such as those of the Norse and Native American Creek. It is therefore offered that the "breath" of spiritual nourishment received in contemplation is most crucial to the vitality of our Craft.

Our tradition has a history of leaders who were not only skilled at running a fraternity and preserving its customs, but were also scholars, philosophers, and seekers of spiritual inspiration and illumination. Without them, the mystic temple of the Craft would never have been more than a fanciful façade, too fragile and hollow to withstand the test of time and the storms of suspicion, prejudice, condemnation, and persecution. Our most inspirational leaders have known and have helped others discover that the breath or light of Masonry does not actually originate from its rituals, symbols, and allegories. They have shown by their own examples that Masonic light is something we must find and develop within ourselves, using the external forms and implements of the Builder's Art as catalysts and tools to help us perform that internal work. The current era is certainly no exception to our ongoing need for such deeply thoughtful, spiritually insightful, and competent leaders. This chapter therefore provides a theoretical design for Masonic contemplative leadership and examines the ethics, skills, and characteristics necessary to those who would help us employ that design by nurturing the mind and spirit as well as the body of our Craft.

DESIGNS ON A TRESTLE BOARD

Three categories of contemplative leadership in the Craft arise from further insight about the three essential areas of Masonic fraternal experience: *membership*, which is primarily concerned with belonging; *instruction*, which is about understanding; and *initiation*, which is concerned with transformation. While the three areas all interact with each other, ritual is regarded as their center of union because that is where they are all begun, repeatedly exemplified, and explained in our common fraternal experience. There are also three kinds of mentoring relationships respectively aligning with those areas: companionship, teaching, and initiating. We now consider that three categories of contemplative leadership – advocacy, consulting, and facilitating – correspond to the overlaps among pairs in the three areas of fraternal experience *(see figure below)*. Advocates are inspiring companions who persuasively promote contemplative practice as a fitting, beneficial, and transformative part of the Masonic experience. Consultants are experienced and well-informed companions who listen and give helpful information and guidance about inner work. Facilitators instructively conduct contemplative activities for the illumination and transformation of members lives.

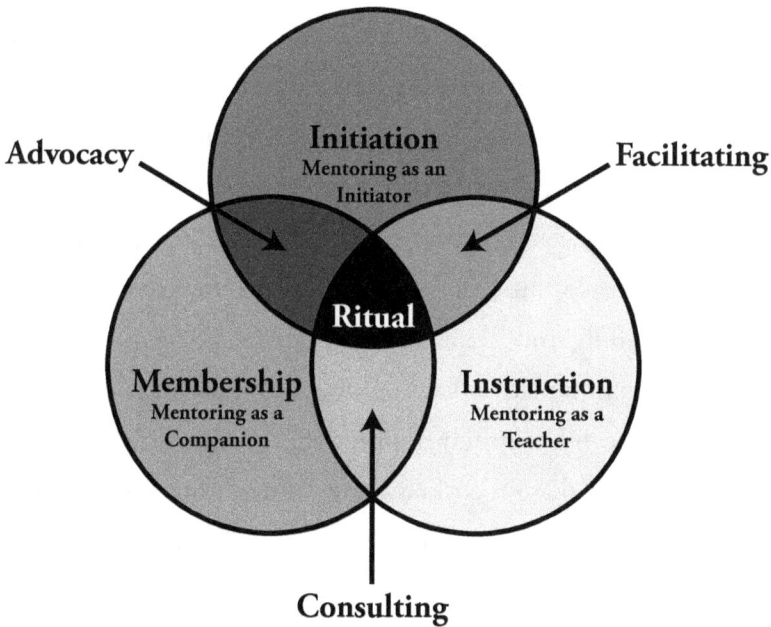

Trestle Board of Masonic Contemplative Leadership

ETHICAL PILLARS

In preparing for and serving their roles, advocates, consultants, and facilitators should include two particular ethical principles as pillars essential to supporting a proper understanding and performance of their responsibilities. The first ethical pillar is respecting and promoting the autonomy of other Masons to make their own judgments and determinations about what is right for them. In the language of the Builder's Art, this ethic is about keeping things on the Level. The second ethical pillar is confidentiality, which the Craft traditionally refers to as secrecy. By keeping the trust of others who confide in them, Masonic contemplative leaders are following the Plumb's lesson to be upright and true.

Regarding the first ethical pillar, leaders of all sorts are often in the position of being hailed as experts, and therefore may be expected to have answers when questions arise. Furthermore, the prestige of being esteemed as an authority and having one's opinions deemed especially valuable, can pose significant temptations to play the part of a dispenser of wisdom. Ethical leaders do their best to meet such moments mindfully and honestly. With questions regarding technical matters of contemplative practice, or about Masonic ritual, customs, or history, it can be entirely appropriate for Masonic contemplative leaders to freely share their knowledge and opinions. However, conscientious leaders are cautious when responding to questions about more subjective matters such as the meanings of others' experiences, their specific moral or spiritual beliefs, their relationships, or their goals for personal growth and transformation. In these cases, rather than give advice or persuade others to adopt any particular view, ethical leaders are mindful that their responsibility is to assist others in exploring such things for themselves. They realize that carefully examining those sorts of questions and responding to them with more questions and options to consider, does more to support others in developing their own best insights and understandings. In short, ethical contemplative leaders diligently honor and encourage the right and the responsibility of others to draft and follow their own designs for who they are and how they live.

Due to their fraternal obligations and their commitment to inner work, contemplative leaders in the Craft are sometimes automatically trusted by groups and individuals with very sensitive information. While speaking of their inner work, people can share the most private things about which they feel guilty, ashamed, anxious, fearful, distrustful, hateful, or resentful. Likewise, both individuals and groups may reveal activities or plans that they prefer to share with others at their own discretion. In many cases, both kinds of disclosures can happen without any notice that they are being made in confidence. Ethical leaders therefore strive to recognize such moments as they arise. They do not assume confidentiality is waived when not requested, and whenever possible they verify whether or not confidentiality is desired by those who have made potentially sensitive disclosures. By honoring confidentiality, Masonic contemplative leaders earn trust and make themselves worthy of helping others with the most significant challenges of their inner work.

BASIC QUALIFICATIONS

While each form of contemplative leadership has its own special qualifications, there are three shared by all of them: authenticity, empathy, and communication skills. These qualifications should be considered indispensable and thus worthy of careful consideration and diligent development before attempting to specialize as an advocate, consultant, or facilitator.

AUTHENTICITY

Definitions for *authentic* use words such as *genuine, trustworthy, real, valid,* and *legitimate*. The word's etymological roots further suggest a degree of authority gained through one's own being and doing.[28] In the present context, authenticity in Masonic contemplative leadership entails possession of relevant knowledge and skills; one must genuinely know what one is talking about. Authentic advocates, consultants, and facilitators alike have given noteworthy effort in learning more about the theory, history, and systems of Masonry and contemplation. Furthermore, they have actual experience in the practices of Masonry and contemplation, which is to say they have developed the invaluable knowledge and skills that come from repeatedly doing something, reflecting on the experiences, and refining both understanding and performance. Without such background development, Masons wishing to be contemplative leaders risk being ineffectual, confusing, misleading, and even destructive, no matter how enthusiastic, sincere, or well-intended they may be.

Most Masons have access to numerous opportunities for gaining more Masonic knowledge and skills through participation in fraternal events and study of the Craft's extensive body of literature. Thus, one's authenticity as a Mason, and even as a Masonic leader, can be built and enhanced through many traditional means.

---

28. Online Etymology Dictionary, https://www.etymonline.com/word/authentic, accessed 2019.

By contrast, achieving authenticity as a contemplative, becoming truly experienced with inner work, has typically required studies and practice outside our fraternal milieu.[29] The Craft therefore needs more members to lead by example in developing as contemplatives, openly sharing those interests and efforts, and explaining to others how their inner work enhances their lives as Masons. By doing so, they not only present themselves more genuinely to their peers, they also assist with contemplative practice becoming widely recognized as a valid aspect of the Builder's Art. Over time, this will help with the expansion of opportunities for distinctly Masonic contemplative instruction and practice, and thus future generations of Masons will not be required to look outside the Craft for initiation, companionship, and teaching in inner work.

EMPATHY

In addition to being personally accomplished, contemplative leaders in the Craft must also be able to relate well with others. Central to this ability is the capacity to empathize, which is recognizing what others feel and using reason to make sense of those feelings, understanding them as clearly as possible. Simply put, empathy is important because emotions are important. An intrinsic part of consciousness, emotions are quite literally *e-motive*; they are forms of energy that *motivate* us, putting our thoughts *in motion* and

29. The author currently knows of only one officially recognized organization dedicated to the study and practice of contemplation in Masonry – the Academy of Reflection. See https://academyofreflection.org, accessed 2019. However, between the writing of this book and its publication, the Masonic Legacy Society has arisen as a worthy grassroots educational effort to introduce and support contemplative practice in Masonry. See https://masoniclegacysociety2026.com/, accessed 2021.

moving us to take action. Like all forms of energy, emotions carry information, revealing useful clues about the conditions that gave rise to them and indicating the possible directions they can take and effects they might have. With empathy, we more clearly perceive the movement and meaning of such energy in others, better comprehending how and why they regard things as desirable or undesirable, agreeable or disagreeable, pleasant or unpleasant. Without empathy our potentials for caring, compassion, fairness, trusting, and being trustworthy are severely diminished. Empathy has thus been at the heart of our evolution as a species, enabling us to form and sustain mutually beneficial relationships – everything from the relatively isolated closeness of personal friendships to the increasing interpersonal complexities of families, teams of coworkers, religious and philanthropic organizations, local communities, nations, and humanity as a whole.

In a very real sense, to be human is to be empathic, and since Masonry aims at making us better humans, it is incumbent upon us to develop our capacity to perceive and comprehend others' feelings. In the Craft, we speak of circumscribing our desires and subduing our passions, keeping them within due bounds, divesting ourselves of vices, practicing virtues, and spreading the cement of brotherly love and affection; each of these labors directly involves emotion.[30] Yet we must clearly see and grasp anything we wish to manage well. Thus, logically speaking, we are less effective in the Builder's Art if we ignore the power and information within emotions, which

---

30. For more on working with emotions in a Masonic context, see Dunning, *Contemplative Masonry*, pp. 136-143.

is even truer when doing inner work together, contemplatively digging into the quarries of our souls and opening them to one another. Consultants, facilitators, and advocates of Masonic contemplative practice must therefore make good use of empathy, demonstrating not only awareness and understanding of others' feelings, but also respecting the significance of those feelings.

The practice of empathy involves using a broad scope of consciousness, including the five senses, emotional feelings, thinking, and intuiting. This is an important point, because people vary in how they naturally use those faculties when relating with others. In any case, empathy is possible for anyone to practice at any time, and to develop one's fullest potentials with empathy requires intentionally engaging all one's faculties in perceiving and understanding the emotions of others. Aspiring leaders for group inner work therefore make empathy an intentional part of their personal contemplative practice. They do so through their studies and the application of mindfulness, contemplative discourse, and discursive meditation, each focused on the nature of emotion and the words, tones of voice, facial expressions, and other ways people communicate their feelings.[31]

COMMUNICATION SKILLS

In the Fellowcraft Degree, among the Liberal Arts and Sciences is the trivium of grammar, rhetoric, and logic. As a qualification for contemplative leadership, rhetoric is chief among the trivium

---

31. For more on empathy and related emotional skills, see Bradberry, Travis and Greaves, Jean, *Emotional Intelligence 2.0*, TalentSmart, 2009; and McLaren, Karla, *The Art of Empathy: A Complete Guide to Life's Most Essential Skill*, Sounds True, 2013.

because it represents the effective integration of grammar and logic in speech. As our rituals and monitors put it:

> *It is by Rhetoric that the art of speaking eloquently is acquired. To be an eloquent speaker, in the proper sense of the word, is far from being either a common, or an easy attainment: it is the art of being persuasive and commanding; the art, not only of pleasing the fancy, but of speaking both to the understanding and to the heart.*[32]

In this reference to the heart, we also see the importance of empathy to the effective communication of contemplative leaders in the Craft; such leaders must discern what is in the hearts of their hearers if they are to consistently touch and move those hearts. A key skill of effective communication is therefore *active listening*, which is far more than passively attending to the words someone says. Whether with groups or individuals, active listeners actually invite and encourage others to speak their hearts and minds. They carefully observe body language, knowing it communicates much more than the words alone. Active listeners paraphrase and summarize others' statements, reflecting back their attitudes, ideas, beliefs, desires, feelings, and questions, and thereby offer others opportunities to confirm or revise how they are being heard and understood. Furthermore, active listeners check their own assumptions, avoid jumping to conclusions, and instead thoughtfully raise questions, seeking more information and clarification in order to more completely and precisely understand others.

32. Atwood, p. 57.

The value of active listening for contemplative leaders in the Craft cannot be overstated. In some cases, their work will meet significant political and psychosocial challenges, and their success in navigating through those challenges will largely be determined by how effectively they have listened and responded to others. By listening in the ways described, contemplative leaders communicate the importance of others as whole human beings, not merely audience members to be lectured, doubters to be convinced, or followers to be recruited and directed. They reveal themselves as servants acting in good faith, working with others to gather valuable information for setting goals and determining how best to serve them. They build feelings of respect, connection, and trust that encourage others to partner with them in that service.

The more leaders listen to others, the better prepared they are to empathically employ the art of rhetoric. But effective rhetoric also requires speakers to provide information and perspectives that help others see and do things differently than they otherwise might. For Masonic contemplative advocates, consultants, and facilitators, this involves guiding other Masons in looking deeper into the allegorical Builder's Art as it is espoused in our rituals and literature. It includes helping others gain greater comprehension of and appreciation for the profound psychological, social, and spiritual implications of the Craft's traditional principles and practices. To be genuinely convincing, the rhetoric of our contemplative leaders is well informed through their own studies and practice as Masons and as contemplatives. To truly engage their listeners, they not only share scholarly insight, but also make themselves relatable by telling their own stories of Masonic inner work and how it has challenged and benefitted them. They speak from their hearts, allowing their passion and love for Masonic light to be clearly seen and heard, thus resonating with and amplifying those sentiments in the hearts of other Masons. Finally, they weave inspiring visions, painting beautiful pictures with words about how contemplative practice helps us, both individually and collectively, to fulfill the noble promises and wonderful potentials of the Builder's Art.

SPECIALIZATION

The following sections of this chapter provide a closer look at the three roles of contemplative leadership. Attention is given to the specific functions of each role, as well as consideration of how each differs in applying the basic qualifications. In the process, it should be kept in mind that these roles are not entirely separate from each other. Anyone acting in one role will often be called upon to serve one or both of the others, and at times may do so simultaneously. The following paragraphs present opportunities for Masons to reflect on how their personal strengths, experiences, and passions might uniquely qualify them to specialize in these roles, as well as consider how their knowledge and skills might be developed across the board.

ADVOCACY

Contemplative advocacy is the effort to promote and encourage inner work through speaking and writing. Referring back to the Trestle Board of Masonic Contemplative Leadership, a contemplative advocate is a *companion initiator* who offers a vision, is inspirational in reminding us of the wonderous possibilities of Masonry, tactfully challenges us to acknowledge our shortcomings, and encourages us to seek transformation and fulfill our potentials. Communication skills are therefore the mainstay of advocacy, which may be called upon in service to groups or individuals considering the possibility of a more contemplative experience of the Builder's Art. Even so, what and how they communicate must be supported by authentic knowledge and an empathic awareness of who they are speaking with.

Advocates for Masonic inner work are genuinely active Masons, thoroughly familiar with our ritual, symbolism, customs, and organizational systems. They are fluent with the language of the Craft, and adept at restating the teachings of our rituals and monitors in contemporary terms relevant to contemplative practice. Furthermore, they anticipate objections and arguments, and are prepared to welcome them graciously, listen empathically, and respond with respectful yet effective counterpoints grounded in Masonic tradition and literature. In all these ways, advocates affirm and assure that contemplative practice is a natural and honorable aspect of Masonry itself, rather than something borrowed from elsewhere.

While authentic knowledge in contemplative practice is especially vital for consultants and facilitators, it is also important for advocates to be familiar with it. Advocates should have enough study or practice with inner work to truthfully extol its benefits to individuals, groups, the Craft as a whole, and beyond. Because they are empathic listeners, advocates employ their knowledge to explain how contemplation is useful in addressing the actual needs and concerns of other Masons. In doing so, they speak in plain terms and use practical examples, helping to ensure that inner work is recognized as a valuable catalyst for transformation, and thus for bringing more wisdom, strength, and beauty to Masons' lives.

Consulting

The responsibility of consultants is to accompany others doing inner work and help them get the most out of it. On the Trestle Board of Masonic Contemplative Leadership, they are shown as *companion instructors*. They are teachers and confidants for whom authenticity as highly informed and seasoned practitioners is paramount, because they are called upon to actually advise other practitioners in navigating their contemplative experiences, understanding them, benefitting from them, and making adjustments in their practice.

Within consultancy, there are two further specializations to consider: working with lodges or other Masonic groups, and focusing on individuals. Those assisting groups require a more extensive background with the Craft's organizational systems and practices, because groups are more likely to need assistance with ethically managing legal and political challenges. At best, group consultants have directly observed and contributed to the successful management of other Masonic contemplative groups and are thus also intimately familiar with group dynamics. In contrast, consultants working with individuals need more experience dealing with the technicalities of solitary contemplative practice, including its personal psychosocial challenges. Because there is no standard course for Masonic inner work, individual consultants should also have a working familiarity with a diverse array of contemplative methods. In both specializations, good consultants maintain active networks with others who have the expertise they lack and are thus able to reach out to their own consultants or make appropriate referrals for their consultees.

Of all the roles of contemplative leadership, consultants are the ones most likely to be trusted with people's secrets, and they are also the ones most likely to be tempted to try solving others' personal dilemmas. Conscientious consultants therefore practice deep self-awareness, seeking out and managing anything within themselves that might lead to a violation of either ethical pillar – confidentiality or respect for autonomy. They regard the confidence of others as a great honor and privilege, one that deserves to be met with utmost care, compassion, and self-discipline. When a sensitive disclosure is made, they intentionally listen with empathy, mindful of the risks being taken by, as well as the faith, hope, and courage of, the one making the disclosure. They recognize such moments are often opportunities for deeper contemplative practice, and thus consultants may encourage others to take advantage of those moments and offer instruction on ways to do so. That approach is especially important when the disclosure concerns a lack of awareness or understanding, or an uncertainty related to a group or individual's self-concept, beliefs, morals, or aspirations. In these circumstances, consultants might occasionally find it helpful to sparingly offer feedback in the form of their own observations, but doing so without judgments or expectations, and with the aim of providing others with more information and options to consider in forming their own opinions and making their own decisions.

FACILITATING

Facilitators are *instructor initiators* who lead experiences of contemplative practice, guiding others through them in ways that present immediate opportunities for inner work and transformation. With regard to the basic qualifications of contemplative leadership, the facilitator role is complex and requires a balance of authenticity, empathy, and communication skills. Furthermore, compared with advocates and consultants, the particular communication skills they employ are more highly specialized.[33]

Facilitate literally means to make something easy.[34] Thus, a facilitator of contemplation has the intention and skills to help others more easily experience contemplative states of consciousness, learn the processes that lead to or enhance those states, and discover how to use them for specific purposes. For groups or individuals, facilitators provide all sorts of activities for inner work, such as contemplative discourse, silent sitting, discursive meditation, guided imagery, and energy work. They ensure that the setting is as conducive as possible to the intended activity, provide participants with prior information and instruction as needed, adeptly use their voices to lead participants through performance of the activity, and afterward may moderate discussion of the experience. As authentic practitioners themselves, facilitators are intimately familiar with the activities they lead and the common effects of those activities. This enables them to

---

33. Due to the uniqueness and complexity of the facilitator role, a thorough set of instructions for developing its skills is provided in Appendix A.

34. *Online Etymology Dictionary*, https://www.etymonline.com/word/facilitate, accessed 2019.

smoothly proceed through all the necessary steps, and it also helps prepare them to empathize with and understand the experiences of others.

The communication skills required for good contemplative facilitation are not often well developed in the ordinary experience of most people. Aspiring facilitators of inner work therefore practice speaking clearly, using volume, tone, and pacing in ways that assist participants in relaxing, centering, and making other shifts of consciousness. They develop the ability to provide instructions without mispronouncing, misusing, or misplacing words, and without sounding mechanical or awkward. Whether using scripts or not, they have rehearsed or previously led the given activities frequently enough to naturally flow from step to step within the allotted time. In reflective dialogue after contemplative activities, facilitators use various techniques to encourage and empathically manage open discussion, thus helping individuals and groups begin making useful sense of their experiences while they are still fresh in their memories.

QUESTIONS FOR FURTHER CONTEMPLATION OF CONTEMPLATIVE LEADERSHIP

- Considering the ethical pillar of respect for autonomy, how would you assess your own tendencies with regard to reflecting rather than judging, and supporting rather than steering, the attitudes, beliefs, and decisions of others?

- Under what circumstances might you be most tempted to exercise uninvited influence on someone's self-concept, morality, or decision making?

- Considering the ethical pillar of confidentiality, how would you assess your past performance in recognizing and conscientiously honoring the sensitive disclosures of others?

- Under what circumstances might you find it ethically justifiable to violate someone's trust?

- How do your values, interests, natural abilities, and previous experiences in and outside the fraternity align with the basic qualifications – authenticity, empathy, and communication skills – of contemplative leadership?

- Regarding the roles of advocacy, consulting, and facilitating, what possibilities do you see for yourself?

- For you, what qualifications for these roles need more development, and how might you do that?

- Among your Masonic associates and acquaintances, who is qualified to serve in each of the three roles, or might become interested in doing so?

AFTERWORD

AFTERWORD

Dear reader, I want to wrap things up by again addressing you more personally. As I write this, I'm sitting on my back porch, happy for the cool air on a morning of what will surely become another scorching Texas August day. I've already been awake for a while and just came out with my cup of coffee after some contemplative practice and a few morning chores. Settling into my purpose in this moment, I feel your presence here with me in a way, and I want you to know how welcome you are and how pleasant it is to know I'm being welcomed by you.

The rest of the manuscript for this manual was completed and sent to the publisher months ago, and ever since then I've had the feeling that it just wasn't quite done. That's not a new feeling for me, because I relate to basically everything I write as a work in progress and never beyond improvement. In this case, I felt there was something else that might be said in *The Contemplative Lodge*, but I found myself resisting the notion of a typical conclusion with a summary of what I'd already written. Then, in the midst of a contemplative moment, I realized that I wanted to say more about the "why" of this book, the deeper motives and intentions for writing it.

To that end, let me share a little story. About two weeks ago, my wife and I were at a cabin in the lovely Hocking Hills region of Ohio, vacationing with another couple who have been dear friends for many years. We've taken lots of camping trips together and share a mutual love of hiking, campfire time, playing games, and talking about life. My daily pattern has been to rise earlier than the others, find a place in the woods, and take time for solitary contemplative practice. On the Ohio trip, my morning contemplations were spent on our cabin's back porch. It jutted out over the hillside, enfolded by pines and oaks that formed a canopy of green, gray, and brown. Each morning I sat there, watching the early rays of the sun penetrate the humid air, caress the boughs and trunks, and alight onto the forest floor.

As I often do in such moments, I recalled Masonry's teaching that we should contemplate the beauties and harmonies of Nature. On one of those mornings my attention was drawn to the vibrant complexity of everything, The crickets' nighttime chorus faded away as the birds sang their awakening, and it all flowed in cycles, with the light of the sun prompting different species to play different parts in different movements through Nature's one continuous composition. What I was appreciating in that moment was the interconnection of everything, the interdependence of being that Nature constantly displays – *everything exists in relationship with everything else.*

The basic reason we hold Geometry of symbolic importance is because it describes how things are related to each other. Geometry is essential to understanding the shape of a crystal, the growth of a snail's shell, the apparent movement of celestial bodies, or the construction of a temple. We are taught that Geometry is, in a speculative sense, synonymous with Masonry, which suggests an analogy: Just as Geometry is about discerning and describing relationships among things in the three dimensions of physical existence, so the Builder's Art is about discerning and describing relationships among things in the various dimensions of social and spiritual existence.

So, Masonry is meant to be the Craft of relationships, and it therefore concerns itself with the relationships among the parts within one's own psyche, the relationships between individual people, relationships within and between groups, with other creatures, and with the Divine. This makes perfect sense to me because relationship is essential to our existence. None of us would be here in this world were it not for relationship: We were conceived in the relationship of our parents; gestated and birthed in the relationship with our mothers; we were nurtured, educated, and developed in relationships with family, friends, and teachers; and we manifest our potentials as adults within a vast and complex myriad of human and non-human relationships. Even the most basic requirements of our continuing survival, such as eating and breathing, depend upon the proper maintenance of many different relational factors. Furthermore, after death, the memories and other effects of our lives continue in the relationships of others.

Ruminating on all of this during one of those mornings in Ohio, I also considered the many angles of relevance to *The Contemplative Lodge*. I realized that everything I've meant to accomplish with this book fits within a context of deeper understandings, experiences, and expressions of relationship. It then dawned on me to submit these reflections for your consideration.

Please keep in mind that I am not denying the importance of our self-realization and self-actualization as individual beings. As I have indicated, the relationships among one's own psychological and spiritual parts are included, and perhaps foremost, among all the others we should contemplate and develop. However, as we do so we cannot fail to eventually observe that even the deepest or most hidden parts of ourselves are affected by our external relationships, and vice versa. It seems patently clear to me that Masonry acknowledges as much. Therefore, to avoid attending to our Craft in either the internal or external dimensions of our lives is an injustice to ourselves, to others, and to the Builder's Art.

There is another word traditionally used in our rituals that illuminates the essence of relationship as well as its greatest potentials, and that word is *love*. Whether we are speaking of the Principal Tenet of Brotherly Love, the Theological Virtue of Charity (*caritas* in Latin, *agape* in Greek), or the sense of pleasant camaraderie spread by the symbolic Trowel, our Craft repeatedly draws our attention to love, welcomes us to dive more deeply into its mysteries, and admonishes us to embody it more fully in the architecture of our lives.

Finally, I am convinced that the reason we set our meeting spaces apart from the profane world is because they are meant to be schools for contemplating and practicing our inner and outer relationships as sacred acts of love. We need tyled spaces for this work simply because the world often seems unconcerned with, if not actively hostile toward, those ends. We need the thresholds and rituals of such spaces to help us make the shifts necessary to fully open our minds, hearts, and arms to joining for those purposes. Within these spaces, having made those shifts, we have opportunities to empower ourselves and each other to then apply the loving art of sacred relationships back out in the profane world, thereby doing our parts to help make ourselves and the world wiser, stronger, and more beautiful. This great work is why we need contemplative lodges and contemplative leaders.

Warm regards,
Chuck Dunning

APPENDICES

APPENDICES

These appendices contain detailed instructions for the development of good facilitation skills along with a series of scripts corresponding to various activities previously described in this book. Unless you are already a skilled contemplative facilitator, begin with a diligent study of Appendix A. Even if you are experienced, it would be worthwhile to at least read through Appendix A to familiarize yourself with the format of facilitation used in most of the scripts.

Each script includes a complete set of instructions for all phases and steps for the given activity. Become thoroughly familiar with a script before using it to facilitate an activity. Notes and additional guidelines for the facilitator appear in italics, and spoken parts are indicated by a regular font. While the scripts are written for groups, they can easily be adapted for individuals. When facilitating an activity with one of the scripts, you should have first practiced reading it aloud enough times to be confident in managing your tone, diction, and pacing, and to know about how long it will take to complete. In general, your group should have about an hour set aside for the entire process of introducing, performing, and reflecting on each activity provided in these appendices. Also note that all scripts are appropriate for use with Masons of any degree.

You are welcome to scan, copy, or otherwise reproduce these scripts for private use. With all but the script for silent sitting, they can be easily adapted for contemplation of focal points other than those presented. Finally, you are asked to verbally cite the source when using one of these scripts to facilitate an activity.

Appendix A:
Facilitator Skills Development

Facilitating group inner work carries significant responsibilities, and so it should never be taken lightly. For example, one never knows when something that seems simple or routine to oneself can be profoundly deep and groundbreaking for someone else. When acting in this role, it is expected that you faithfully execute your duty to ensure such experiences are ethical and effective. To be as effective as possible, you should conscientiously learn, develop, and hone all the skills necessary to safely and successfully guide others through potentially powerful inner experiences.

Voice Skills

Your voice can have significant effects on the experiences of participants in a contemplative activity. Carefully consider each of the following skills, reflecting on how you may have experienced them while being guided by someone else, whether in person or in a recording. Experiment and practice with these skills, and consider making audio recordings in order to evaluate your performance. Invite others to provide feedback on your voice skills.

TONE

The tone of your voice is expressed in three primary ways — volume, inflection, and diction.

VOLUME

The loudness of your voice should be sufficient to clearly reach everyone in the room, but consider the probability that some participants will not hear as well as others. Ask participants if they can hear you well enough. Be mindful of your volume as you proceed through an activity, ensuring that you maintain a constant level in order for all participants to receive each of your instructions.

INFLECTION

Participants will naturally sense and respond to the emotional energies expressed through your voice. In order to effectively express such energies, you must call upon your own relevant feelings. Therefore, prior to an activity you should consider what feelings will be most conducive to its intentions. Keep in mind that it is not necessary to exaggerate your feelings, in part because in a contemplative state your participants will be more sensitive to them.

1. ***Relaxing and centering*** benefits from a calm, peaceful, soothing quality.
2. ***Proceeding through specific operations*** may require various subtle energies. Would any of the operations benefit from communicating the feelings naturally associated with experiences such as awe, wonder, hopefulness, happiness, puzzlement, or resoluteness?
3. ***Reconnecting with the present*** can be aided by a gently assertive tone.

4. ***Ending the activity*** with an attitude of positivity and a sense of accomplishment helps set the stage for reflection.

DICTION

This skill is about speaking clearly and using good enunciation with appropriate words that are properly pronounced. Regarding word choice, try to use terminology that will be familiar to all participants. Avoid the use of metaphysical lingo or unexplained jargon. For example, unless you know everyone present understands the word *chakra*, use something more descriptive like *energy center*, or simply draw attention to the physical location in a fitting way. With pronunciation, consider the importance of sounding out each syllable rather than blending or slurring them. Strive to moderate any accent or dialectical differences that may habitually be present for you. When following a script, be sure you are familiar with the meaning and pronunciation of *every* word.

PACING

Proceed with all narration at a pace that is slow and steady. Doing so helps in two ways: it establishes a rhythm that helps participants be more attentive to your words and tone; and it enables you to use better diction. Until you've developed a good sense of timing, use a clock, watch, or timer for managing time.

REPETITION

Repeated use of the same words and phrases can assist participants with focusing in the processes you actually intend to facilitate. It also leaves mental space for them to be more aware of what is occurring within them. Using different words with similar meanings or stating things in different ways tends to make people think more about your words, stimulating analytical processes in search of possible implications. This natural reaction can distract participants from smoothly following along in the processes you actually mean to facilitate, but repetition combined with effective pacing has melodic effects that, much like those of music or poetry, can help naturally induce the desired states of consciousness. In some cases, such as in discursive meditation, you may intend for participants to be more analytical about the words being used, and might therefore speak with more spontaneity and variety.

EIGHT STEPS OF GUIDED MEDITATION

There is a natural progression of steps involved in guiding an individual or group through a guided meditation. Contemplate each of the steps below, reflecting on how you may have experienced them when being guided by someone else. Consider the relevance of the two ethical pillars – autonomy and confidentiality – and three basic qualifications for contemplative leadership – authenticity, empathy, and communication skills. As you serve in the facilitator role, from time to time, seek feedback from participants about your skills. These steps are written for group meditations but are easily adapted to assisting an individual.

1. CONSIDER YOUR AUDIENCE

How experienced in meditation are the persons you are serving? What kinds of meditation are or are not familiar to your audience? How much time do they have? Does anyone need to leave early? How will these factors affect your work?

2. PREPARE THE SPACE

Is there enough room? Are the accommodations adequately comfortable with regard to things like seating, temperature, and individual space? What can be done to manage distractions like noise or intrusions? Will you need a clock visible to help you with timing? Will you need time and materials to perform a ritual cleansing, consecration, or invocation for the space?

3. WELCOME PARTICIPANTS

Thank everyone for coming and state it is time to focus on meditation. Ask for cell phones to be completely silenced and set an example by letting others see you doing so. Ask if you are speaking loudly enough for everyone to clearly hear you.

4. PROVIDE INTRODUCTIONS AS NEEDED

Unless you are certain everyone knows you, tell them your name, your connection with the fraternity, and that you will be facilitating the meditation for this session. Consider whether or not it would be helpful and time-efficient to welcome participants to introduce themselves.

5. EXPLAIN WHAT TO EXPECT

Briefly describe the purpose or focal point of the meditation. How detailed do you want to be about the specific operations? Could

more detail or less detail enhance the experience? Consider inform-
ing participants of any connection the meditation may have with
specific elements of their Masonic experience, such as particular degrees, themes, or symbols. With beginners, provide instruction on
how to respond to distractions whether external, such as latecomers
entering the room, or internal, such as thoughts going off on tan-
gents. You might also wish to address the myths about meditation
and offer basic instruction on good meditation posture. Consider
stating that closing eyes is recommended but not required, and that
gazing blankly at some fixed point is an option. If you are using a
script, state the source. Ask if there are any questions.

6. Narrate Meditation Through Four Phases

Relaxing and Centering

Invite participants to begin by silently invoking the aid of Deity. Narrate a progressive relaxation technique and then guide the
group in focusing on breathing. With a group of experienced practitioners, you might invite them to guide themselves through this
phase, and then allow a suitable period of silence.

Proceeding Through Specific Operations

It is preferable to narrate the specific operations from memory,
but a script may be used if necessary. If a script is used, you should
have carefully read through it and practiced it aloud enough that you
can proceed smoothly with good diction. Also, with a paper script,
be careful to turn pages as quietly as possible.

RECONNECTING WITH THE PRESENT

With most meditations, it is wise to guide participants into re-grounding with focusing on the breath and awareness of the five senses. In some cases, less attention is given to this phase in order to remain in or closer to a certain state of consciousness.

ENDING THE MEDITATION

State that the meditation has ended. Prompt participants to open their eyes, move, and stretch their limbs.

7. FACILITATE REFLECTION WITH FIVE SKILLS

WELCOMING SHARING

Advise participants that they are welcome to offer anything they wish about their own experiences of the meditation, such as: new insights; puzzling, unusual, or problematic moments; and questions. Ask everyone to remain mindful that there are others in the room who may need space and time to speak. Offer words of encouragement and thanks when people speak, especially on the first occurrence. With groups where participants are hesitant to share, consider offering an explanation of the practical benefits of translating our experiences into language. You may wish to set an example by being the first to speak about your own experience with the meditation.

ACTIVE LISTENING

Listen to understand, which means not distracting yourself with thoughts about what you might say when someone stops talking. Empathically attend to the emotions of participants. Be cautious about assuming what someone means or needs. Consider restating the speaker's points or questions in your own words to confirm you understood. Ask questions to gain clarity. Point out similarities among things different participants have said, which builds the sense of belonging and congruence in the group.

Scanning the Group

Avoid focusing too much attention on the person speaking. Use both your direct line of sight and your peripheral vision to be aware of other individuals in the group. Watch for non-verbal cues, such as raising hands, nodding or shaking heads, cocked heads, or changes in facial expressions. Allow it to be obvious that you are trying to be mindful of everyone.

Managing the Flow

Use the questions of the W^3 technique presented in Chapter 2 to advance the group through the phases of reflection. As you scan the group, follow up on cues that someone might have something to say, especially with those who haven't yet spoken. If one or a few participants seem to be dominating the conversation, respond to the cues of less outspoken individuals by directly inviting them to share their experiences, thoughts, and feelings. Be mindful that participants can be fully engaged with the group's reflections, even though they are silent and seem detached, and may benefit by not being disturbed. If someone declines to speak when asked, honor that choice.

Being Careful with Advice

Avoid giving unrequested advice. Your role is not to be a guru, spiritual advisor, therapist, or life coach. Know that the best response to requests for feedback or advice is often to put such questions back to the participants, asking how they might respond if such were asked of them. On simple matters of technique, you may be able to easily offer helpful tips. You may also be able to recommend specific methods for specific purposes, offering options rather than prescribing solutions to others' needs. Avoid issuing judgments about others' practices or experiences. Be quick to acknowledge your lack of knowledge or experience with any practice, system, or tradition. If you offer an opinion, then clearly state it as such. Make it a point to welcome the input of someone particular in the group whom you trust to be more informed on any point of discussion. In addition to exercising these cautions with yourself, you should also be mindful of and responsive to advice-giving behaviors of others in the group. Intervene and redirect as necessary.

8. WRAP UP AND CLOSE

Announce that it is time to end the session. Restate some of the more common or poignant reflections. Inform them about the next time and location for meditation or other contemplative activities. Thank everyone for their participation.

APPENDIX B:
CONTEMPLATIVE DISCOURSE SCRIPTS

DISCOURSE SCRIPT #1: INITIATION

Become thoroughly familiar with this script before using it to facilitate an activity. Notes and additional guidelines for the facilitator appear in italics, and spoken parts are indicated by a regular font. Consider your audience and what, if any, adjustments you might make in facilitating this activity. Ensure that the space is appropriately prepared.

WELCOME PARTICIPANTS

Thank everyone for coming and state that it is time to focus on contemplative discourse. Ask for cell phones to be completely silenced and set an example by letting others see you doing so. Ask if you are speaking loudly enough for everyone to clearly hear you.

PROVIDE INTRODUCTIONS AS NEEDED

Unless you are certain everyone knows you, tell them your name, your connection with the fraternity, and that you will be facilitating the contemplative discourse. Consider whether or not it would be helpful and time-efficient to welcome participants to introduce themselves.

EXPLAIN WHAT TO EXPECT

In this session, I am following a script from *The Contemplative Lodge: A Manual for Masons Doing Inner Work Together*, and we will have discourse on the topic of initiation. The practice of contemplative discourse offers participants the opportunity to join in reverent, mutually supportive exploration of the symbols, teachings, and experiences of our Craft. This process always involves at least one of two types of thinking – reflection and speculation – both of which are intimately interwoven with our common fraternal experiences. As we explore possibilities, we should understand and respect the difference between traditional meanings and personal meanings for our symbols and teachings. Traditional meanings are those specified in our rituals and monitors, or those from other sources that are widely agreed upon within the fraternity and have stood the test of time. Personal meanings result from an individual's own studies, contemplations, and other experiences, and they may significantly diverge from traditional meanings. Both kinds of meaning are valid within their own contexts. We therefore proceed with the affirmation that no individual or organization within the Craft has the right to demand that Masons limit their personal understandings to the traditional meanings, just as individuals should not expect their personal meanings be approved or adopted by others. And, while an openness to different perspectives and understandings is vital to contemplative discourse, so is the effort to carefully examine concepts, clarify our thinking about them, and consider their usefulness for improving our lives or the lives of others. After some time for relaxation and centering, I will state the focal point for this session, and after a brief period of meditation, we will begin the discourse. Are there any questions?

RELAXATION AND CENTERING

Closing your eyes or gazing blankly at some point in front of you, begin to relax and turn your attention inward. If you wish, take a moment to silently invoke the aid of Deity.

Pause for several breaths.

Slowly take in a deep breath, inhaling all the air you can without straining, and then hold it, hold it, hold it. Now release the breath, exhaling all the air you can without straining, and then pause, pause, pause.

Slowly take in a second deep breath, inhaling all the air you can without straining, and then hold it, hold it, hold it. Now release the breath, exhaling all the air you can without straining, and then pause, pause, pause.

Slowly take in a third deep breath, inhaling all the air you can without straining, and then hold it, hold it, hold it. Now release the breath, exhaling all the air you can without straining, and then pause, pause, pause. Now inhale and let your body breathe in its own peaceful, natural rhythm.

Pause for a few breaths.

FOCAL POINT

Our focal point for this session is the word initiation. Concentrate on the word initiation, making it the central point within the circle of your thoughts and feelings about initiation.

Pause for several breaths.

DISCOURSE

Now open your eyes and bring your attention back to the group so that we may begin our discourse.

For the allotted time, invite participants to share their experiences, insights, and questions. Remember to use these skills:

- *welcoming sharing*

- *active listening*

- *scanning the group*

- *managing the flow*

- *being careful with advice*

Consider using the following questions to prompt sharing.

- *What seems superficially obvious about the focal point, without any traditional or ritual explanations? How might these simple observations have symbolic or allegorical meaning?*

- *What were the contexts – time, place, and other circumstances – in which you each first experienced the focal point, and how might the contexts affect the meaning?*

- *What thoughts, feelings, or questions first arose for you during the initial moments of experiencing of the focal point? What meanings might they suggest?*

- *How is the focal point identical or similar to other things, whether inside or outside Masonry, and how might the meanings of those things be relevant?*

- *If you open your hearts and minds to the widest range of possibilities, without any concern for being correct or making sense, what hunches, intuitions, inspirations, or questions arise?*

- *How can multiple meanings, or layers of meaning, be simultaneously present for the focal point, even if they seem to contradict each other?*

WRAP UP AND CLOSE

Announce that it is time to end the session. Ask participants to spend a moment in silent reflection on the discourse. After pausing for several breaths, restate some of the more common or poignant reflections and speculations. Inform participants about the next time and location for contemplative discourse or other contemplative activities. Thank everyone for their participation.

DISCOURSE SCRIPT #2: THE BLAZING STAR

Become thoroughly familiar with this script before using it to facilitate an activity. Notes and additional guidelines for the facilitator appear in italics, and spoken parts are indicated by a regular font. Consider your audience and what, if any, adjustments you might make in facilitating this activity. Ensure that the space is appropriately prepared. For the focal point, you may wish to have an image of the Blazing Star in the Mosaic Pavement where everyone can see it:

WELCOME PARTICIPANTS

Thank everyone for coming and state that it is time to focus on contemplative discourse. Ask for cell phones to be completely silenced and set an example by letting others see you doing so. Ask if you are speaking loudly enough for everyone to clearly hear you.

PROVIDE INTRODUCTIONS AS NEEDED

Unless you are certain everyone knows you, tell them your name, your connection with the fraternity, and that you will be facilitating the contemplative discourse. Consider whether or not it would be helpful and time-efficient to welcome participants to introduce themselves.

EXPLAIN WHAT TO EXPECT

In this session, I am following a script from *The Contemplative Lodge: A Manual for Masons Doing Inner Work Together,* and we will have discourse on the Blazing Star. The practice of contemplative discourse offers participants the opportunity to join in reverent, mutually supportive exploration of the symbols, teachings, and experiences of our Craft. This process always involves at least one of two types of thinking – reflection and speculation – both of which are intimately interwoven with our common fraternal experiences. As we explore possibilities, we should understand and respect the difference between traditional meanings and personal meanings for our symbols and teachings. Traditional meanings are those specified in our rituals and monitors, or those from other sources that are widely agreed upon within the fraternity and have stood the test of time. Personal meanings result from an individual's own studies, contemplations, and other experiences, and they may significantly diverge from traditional meanings. Both kinds of meaning are valid within their own contexts. We therefore proceed with the affirmation that no individual or organization within the Craft has the right to demand that Masons limit their personal understandings to the traditional meanings, just as individuals should not expect their personal meanings be approved or adopted by others. And, while an openness to different perspectives and understandings is vital to contemplative discourse, so is the effort to carefully examine things, clarify our thinking about them, and consider their usefulness for improving our lives or the lives of others. After some time for relaxation and centering, I will state the focal point for this session, and after a brief period of meditation, we will begin the discourse. Are there any questions?

RELAXATION AND CENTERING

Closing your eyes or gazing blankly at some point in front of you, begin to relax and turn your attention inward. If you wish, take a moment to silently invoke the aid of Deity.

Pause for several breaths.

Slowly take in a deep breath, inhaling all the air you can without straining, and then hold it, hold it, hold it. Now release the breath, exhaling all the air you can without straining, and then pause, pause, pause.

Slowly take in a second deep breath, inhaling all the air you can without straining, and then hold it, hold it, hold it. Now release the breath, exhaling all the air you can without straining, and then pause, pause, pause.

Slowly take in a third deep breath, inhaling all the air you can without straining, and then hold it, hold it, hold it. Now release the breath, exhaling all the air you can without straining, and then pause, pause, pause. Now inhale and let your body breathe in its own peaceful, natural rhythm.

Pause for a few breaths.

FOCAL POINT

Our focal point for this session is the Blazing Star. Concentrate on the Blazing Star, making it the central point within the circle of your thoughts and feelings about the Blazing Star.

Pause for several breaths.

DISCOURSE

Now open your eyes and bring your attention back to the group so that we may begin our discourse.

For the allotted time, invite participants to share their experiences, insights, and questions. Remember to use these skills:

- *welcoming sharing*

- *active listening*

- *scanning the group*

- *managing the flow*

- *being careful with advice*

Consider using the following questions to prompt sharing.

- *What seems superficially obvious about the focal point, without any traditional or ritual explanations? How might these simple observations have symbolic or allegorical meaning?*

- *What were the contexts – time, place, and other circumstances – in which you each first experienced the focal point, and how might the contexts affect the meaning?*

- *What thoughts, feelings, or questions first arose for you during the initial moments of experiencing of the focal point? What meanings might they suggest?*

- *How is the focal point identical or similar to other things, whether inside or outside Masonry, and how might the meanings of those things be relevant?*

- *If you open your hearts and minds to the widest range of possibilities, without any concern for being correct or making sense, what hunches, intuitions, inspirations, or questions arise?*

- *How can multiple meanings, or layers of meaning, be simultaneously present for the focal point, even if they seem to contradict each other?*

WRAP UP AND CLOSE

Announce that it is time to end the session. Ask participants to spend a moment in silent reflection on the discourse. After pausing for several breaths, restate some of the more common or poignant reflections and speculations. Inform participants about the next time and location for contemplative discourse or other contemplative activities. Thank everyone for their participation.

DISCOURSE SCRIPT #3: THE COMMON GAVEL

Become thoroughly familiar with this script before using it to facilitate an activity. Notes and additional guidelines for the facilitator appear in italics, and spoken parts are indicated by a regular font. Consider your audience and what, if any, adjustments you might make in facilitating this activity. Ensure that the space is appropriately prepared. For the focal point, you may wish to have a gavel where everyone can see and handle it. Try to use something designed like an actual stonemason's gavel rather than the gavels typically used for keeping order in meetings.

WELCOME PARTICIPANTS

Thank everyone for coming and state that it is time to focus on contemplative discourse. Ask for cell phones to be completely silenced and set an example by letting others see you doing so. Ask if you are speaking loudly enough for everyone to clearly hear you.

PROVIDE INTRODUCTIONS AS NEEDED

Unless you are certain everyone knows you, tell them your name, your connection with the fraternity, and that you will be facilitating the contemplative discourse. Consider whether or not it would be helpful and time-efficient to welcome participants to introduce themselves.

EXPLAIN WHAT TO EXPECT

In this session, I am following a script from *The Contemplative Lodge: A Manual for Masons Doing Inner Work Together,* and we will have discourse on the Common Gavel. The practice of contemplative discourse offers participants the opportunity to join in reverent, mutually supportive exploration of the symbols, teachings, and experiences of our Craft. This process always involves at least one of two types of thinking – reflection and speculation – both of which are intimately interwoven with our common fraternal experiences. As we explore possibilities, we should understand and respect the difference between traditional meanings and personal meanings for our symbols and teachings. Traditional meanings are those specified in our rituals and monitors, or those from other sources that are widely agreed upon within the fraternity and have stood the test of time. Personal meanings result from an individual's own studies, contemplations, and other experiences, and they may significantly diverge from traditional meanings. Both kinds of meaning are valid within their own contexts. We therefore proceed with the affirmation that no individual or organization within the Craft has the right to demand that Masons limit their personal understandings to the traditional meanings, just as individuals should not expect their personal meanings be approved or adopted by others. And, while an openness to different perspectives and understandings is vital to contemplative discourse, so is the effort to carefully examine things, clarify our thinking about them, and consider their usefulness for improving our lives or the lives of others. After some time for relaxation and centering, I will state the focal point for this session, and after a brief period of meditation, we will begin the discourse. Are there any questions?

RELAXATION AND CENTERING

Closing your eyes or gazing blankly at some point in front of you, begin to relax and turn your attention inward. If you wish, take a moment to silently invoke the aid of Deity.

Pause for several breaths.

Slowly take in a deep breath, inhaling all the air you can without straining, and then hold it, hold it, hold it. Now release the breath, exhaling all the air you can without straining, and then pause, pause, pause.

Slowly take in a second deep breath, inhaling all the air you can without straining, and then hold it, hold it, hold it. Now release the breath, exhaling all the air you can without straining, and then pause, pause, pause.

Slowly take in a third deep breath, inhaling all the air you can without straining, and then hold it, hold it, hold it. Now release the breath, exhaling all the air you can without straining, and then pause, pause, pause. Now inhale and let your body breathe in its own peaceful, natural rhythm.

Pause for a few breaths.

FOCAL POINT

Our focal point for this session is the Common Gavel. Concentrate on the Common Gavel, making it the central point within the circle of your thoughts and feelings about the Common Gavel.

Pause for several breaths.

DISCOURSE

Now open your eyes and bring your attention back to the group so that we may begin our discourse.

For the allotted time, invite participants to share their experiences, insights, and questions. Remember to use these skills:

- *welcoming sharing*

- *active listening*

- *scanning the group*

- *managing the flow*

- *being careful with advice*

Consider using the following questions to prompt sharing.

- *What seems superficially obvious about the focal point, without any traditional or ritual explanations? How might these simple observations have symbolic or allegorical meaning?*

- *What were the contexts – time, place, and other circumstances – in which you each first experienced the focal point, and how might the contexts affect the meaning?*

- *What thoughts, feelings, or questions first arose for you during the initial moments of experiencing of the focal point? What meanings might they suggest?*

- *How is the focal point identical or similar to other things, whether inside or outside Masonry, and how might the meanings of those things be relevant?*

- *If you open your hearts and minds to the widest range of possibilities, without any concern for being correct or making sense, what hunches, intuitions, inspirations, or questions arise?*

- *How can multiple meanings, or layers of meaning, be simultaneously present for the focal point, even if they seem to contradict each other?*

WRAP UP AND CLOSE

Announce that it is time to end the session. Ask participants to spend a moment in silent reflection on the discourse. After pausing for several breaths, restate some of the more common or poignant reflections and speculations. Inform participants about the next time and location for contemplative discourse or other contemplative activities. Thank everyone for their participation.

APPENDIX C:
GROUP MEDITATION SCRIPTS

Silent Sitting

Become thoroughly familiar with this script before using it to facilitate an activity. Notes and additional guidelines for the facilitator appear in italics, and spoken parts are indicated by a regular font. Consider your audience and what, if any, adjustments you might make in facilitating this activity. With more experienced practitioners, longer periods of silent sitting may be welcome. Ensure that the space is appropriately prepared.

Welcome Participants

Thank everyone for coming and state it is time to focus on meditation. Ask for cell phones to be completely silenced and set an example by letting others see you doing so. Ask if you are speaking loudly enough for everyone to clearly hear you.

Provide Introductions as Needed

Unless you are certain everyone knows you, tell them your name, your connection with the fraternity, and that you will be facilitating the meditation for this session. Consider whether or not it would be helpful and time-efficient to welcome participants to introduce themselves.

Explain What to Expect

In this meditation we will practice silent sitting, and I am following a script from *The Contemplative Lodge: A Manual for Masons Doing Inner Work Together.* It is a myth that silent sitting means having no thoughts or sense perceptions at all. Even experienced meditators notice such things. The silence is the quiet space of consciousness in which those things arise and then disappear. That quiet space of consciousness is always present, and so we are simply practicing awareness of it. Despite its seemingly basic and simple nature, it can also be among the most beneficial of practices, and is thus often the mainstay of inner work for experienced meditators. Are there any questions?

RELAXATION AND CENTERING

Closing your eyes or gazing blankly at some point in front of you, begin to relax and turn your attention inward. If you wish, take a moment to silently invoke the aid of Deity.

Pause for several breaths.

Slowly take in a deep breath, inhaling all the air you can without straining, and then hold it, hold it, hold it. Now release the breath, exhaling all the air you can without straining, and then pause, pause, pause.

Slowly take in a second deep breath, inhaling all the air you can without straining, and then hold it, hold it, hold it. Now release the breath, exhaling all the air you can without straining, and then pause, pause, pause.

Slowly take in a third deep breath, inhaling all the air you can without straining, and then hold it, hold it, hold it. Now release the breath, exhaling all the air you can without straining, and then pause, pause,

pause. Now inhale and let your body breathe in its own peaceful, natural rhythm.

Pause for a couple of breaths.

Attend to the sensation of the earth's gravity pulling down on your body. Feel it pulling your feet against the floor. Feel gravity pulling down in your calves and shins. If you notice any unnecessary tension in those muscles, let it go, and let the pull of gravity take you into a deeper state of calm, peaceful relaxation.

Pause for a couple of breaths.

Feel gravity pulling down in your thighs and buttocks, pulling you into your seat. If you notice any unnecessary tension in those muscles, let it go, and let the pull of gravity take you into a deeper state of calm, peaceful relaxation.

Pause for a couple of breaths.

Feel gravity pulling down in your hips, belly, and lower back. If you notice any unnecessary tension in those muscles, let it go, leaving only what is necessary to keep you sitting in a healthy posture, and let the pull of gravity take you into a deeper state of calm, peaceful relaxation.

Pause for a couple of breaths.

Feel gravity pulling down in your ribcage, chest, and upper back. If you notice any unnecessary tension in those muscles, let it go, leaving only what is necessary to keep you sitting in a healthy posture, and

let the pull of gravity take you into a deeper state of calm, peaceful relaxation.

Pause for a couple of breaths.

Feel gravity pulling down in your shoulders and neck. If you notice any unnecessary tension in those muscles, let it go, leaving only what is necessary to keep you sitting in a healthy posture, and let the pull of gravity take you into a deeper state of calm, peaceful relaxation.

Pause for a couple of breaths.

Feel gravity pulling down in your upper arms, forearms, wrists, and hands. If you notice any unnecessary tension in those muscles, let it go, and let the pull of gravity take you into a deeper state of calm, peaceful relaxation.

Pause for a couple of breaths.

Feel gravity pulling down in your jaw, your tongue, around your mouth, and in your cheeks. Feel gravity pulling down around your eyes and in your brow. Feel gravity pulling down in your scalp on the top of your head, around the sides, and down the back. If you notice any unnecessary tension in those muscles, let it go, leaving only what is necessary to keep you sitting in a healthy posture, and let the pull of gravity take you into a deeper state of calm, peaceful relaxation.

Pause for a couple of breaths.

Now, feel gravity pulling down from the top of your head all the way through every part of your body down to the soles of your feet. If you notice any unnecessary tension anywhere, let it go, leaving only what is necessary to keep you sitting in a healthy posture, and let the pull of gravity take you into a deeper state of calm, peaceful relaxation.

Pause for a couple of breaths.

Turn your attention back to your breath, flowing in and out in its own peaceful, natural rhythm. Simply observe it flowing in and out in its own peaceful, natural rhythm. Feel each breath taking you into a deeper state of calm, peaceful relaxation.

Pause for a few breaths.

You can go into an even deeper state of calm, peaceful relaxation by silently marking the breath with the word "in" as you inhale, and "out" as you exhale: iiiiiinnn, ooouuut. Just continue observing the breath flowing in and out in its own peaceful, natural rhythm as you continue silently repeating: iiiiiinnn, ooouuut. Feel each breath taking you into a deeper state of calm, peaceful relaxation.

Pause for several breaths.

SITTING SILENTLY

Let go of marking the breath with the words in and out. Now is the time to just sit in silent stillness, attending to the quiet space of consciousness in which all thoughts, feelings, and sense perceptions arise and disappear. If you find yourself becoming distracted by such things, gently return your awareness to the silence. It may help to once again focus on the breath, perhaps internally using the words in and out to assist you, and then letting them go to again sit in silent stillness. Patiently repeat this process as often as necessary. Now practice attending to the silence.

Pause for the allotted time.

RECONNECT WITH THE PRESENT AND END THE MEDITATION

Attend to the sensations of your body. Feel gravity pulling you down into your seat and your feet against the floor. Feel the air on your skin and your breath flowing in and out. Hear what you hear. Smell what you smell and taste what you taste. When you are ready, open your eyes and see what you see.

The meditation has ended. Feel free to move and stretch your limbs.

REFLECTION

Invite participants to share their experiences, insights, and questions. Remember to use these skills:

- *welcoming sharing*

- *active listening*

- *scanning the group*

- *managing the flow*

- *being careful with advice*

WRAP UP AND CLOSE

Announce that it is time to end the session. Restate some of the more common or poignant reflections. Inform participants about the next time and location for meditation or other contemplative activities. Thank everyone for their participation.

DISCURSIVE SCRIPT #1: WISDOM, STRENGTH, AND BEAUTY

Become thoroughly familiar with this script before using it to facilitate an activity. Notes and additional guidelines for the facilitator appear in italics, and spoken parts are indicated by a regular font. Consider your audience and what, if any, adjustments you might make in facilitating this activity. You may wish to provide an image of the three pillars traditionally associated with the Principal Supports of the Lodge. Ensure that the space is appropriately prepared.

WELCOME PARTICIPANTS

Thank everyone for coming and state it is time to focus on meditation. Ask for cell phones to be completely silenced and set an example by letting others see you doing so. Ask if you are speaking loudly enough for everyone to clearly hear you.

PROVIDE INTRODUCTIONS AS NEEDED

Unless you are certain everyone knows you, tell them your name, your connection with the fraternity, and that you will be facilitating the meditation for this session. Consider whether or not it would be helpful and time-efficient to welcome participants to introduce themselves.

EXPLAIN WHAT TO EXPECT

In this session, I am following a script from *The Contemplative Lodge: A Manual for Masons Doing Inner Work Together*, and we will practice discursive meditation on the Principal Supports of the Lodge – Wisdom, Strength, and Beauty. Discursive meditation consists of having a deep, contemplative discourse within yourself, using the faculties of association, analysis, intuition, and interactive imagination. I will lead you through the process of doing so. Are there any questions?

RELAXATION AND CENTERING

Closing your eyes or gazing blankly at some point in front of you, begin to relax and turn your attention inward. If you wish, take a moment to silently invoke the aid of Deity.

Pause for several breaths.

Slowly take in a deep breath, inhaling all the air you can without straining, and then hold it, hold it, hold it. Now release the breath, exhaling all the air you can without straining, and then pause, pause, pause.

Slowly take in a second deep breath, inhaling all the air you can without straining, and then hold it, hold it, hold it. Now release the breath, exhaling all the air you can without straining, and then pause, pause, pause.

Slowly take in a third deep breath, inhaling all the air you can without straining, and then hold it, hold it, hold it. Now release the breath, exhaling all the air you can without straining, and then pause, pause,

pause. Now inhale and let your body breathe in its own peaceful, natural rhythm.

Pause for a couple of breaths.

Attend to the sensation of the earth's gravity pulling down on your body. Feel it pulling your feet against the floor. Feel gravity pulling down in your calves and shins. If you notice any unnecessary tension in those muscles, let it go, and let the pull of gravity take you into a deeper state of calm, peaceful relaxation.

Pause for a couple of breaths.

Feel gravity pulling down in your thighs and buttocks, pulling you into your seat. If you notice any unnecessary tension in those muscles, let it go, and let the pull of gravity take you into a deeper state of calm, peaceful relaxation.

Pause for a couple of breaths.

Feel gravity pulling down in your hips, belly, and lower back. If you notice any unnecessary tension in those muscles, let it go, leaving only what is necessary to keep you sitting in a healthy posture, and let the pull of gravity take you into a deeper state of calm, peaceful relaxation.

Pause for a couple of breaths.

Feel gravity pulling down in your ribcage, chest, and upper back. If you notice any unnecessary tension in those muscles, let it go, leaving only what is necessary to keep you sitting in a healthy posture, and let the pull of gravity take you into a deeper state of calm, peaceful relaxation.

Pause for a couple of breaths.

Feel gravity pulling down in your shoulders and neck. If you notice any unnecessary tension in those muscles, let it go, leaving only what is necessary to keep you sitting in a healthy posture, and let the pull of gravity take you into a deeper state of calm, peaceful relaxation.

Pause for a couple of breaths.

Feel gravity pulling down in your upper arms, forearms, wrists, and hands. If you notice any unnecessary tension in those muscles, let it go, and let the pull of gravity take you into a deeper state of calm, peaceful relaxation.

Pause for a couple of breaths.

Feel gravity pulling down in your jaw, your tongue, around your mouth, and in your cheeks. Feel gravity pulling down around your eyes and in your brow. Feel gravity pulling down in your scalp on the top of your head, around the sides, and down the back. If you notice any unnecessary tension in those muscles, let it go, leaving only what is necessary to keep you sitting in a healthy posture, and let the pull of gravity take you into a deeper state of calm, peaceful relaxation.

Pause for a couple of breaths.

Now, feel gravity pulling down from the top of your head all the way through every part of your body down to the soles of your feet. If you notice any unnecessary tension anywhere, let it go, leaving only what is necessary to keep you sitting in a healthy posture, and let the pull of gravity take you into a deeper state of calm, peaceful relaxation.

Pause for a couple of breaths.

Turn your attention back to your breath, flowing in and out in its own peaceful, natural rhythm. Simply observe it flowing in and out in its own peaceful, natural rhythm. Feel each breath taking you into a deeper state of calm, peaceful relaxation.

Pause for a few breaths.

You can go into an even deeper state of calm, peaceful relaxation by silently marking the breath with the word "in" as you inhale, and "out" as you exhale: iiiiiinnn, ooouuut. Just continue observing the breath flowing in and out in its own peaceful, natural rhythm as you continue silently repeating: iiiiiinnn, ooouuut. Feel each breath taking you into a deeper state of calm, peaceful relaxation.

Pause for several breaths.

Discursive Process

We now begin discursive meditation with the focal point of Wisdom, Strength, and Beauty. Make the words Wisdom, Strength, and Beauty the central point within the circle of your thoughts and feelings about Wisdom, Strength, and Beauty. For a moment, simply sit quietly, establishing and holding that focal point within the quiet, still space of your mind.

Pause for a few breaths.

Allow your mind to make associations with the focal point. For you, what ideas, memories, or feelings naturally connect with Wisdom, Strength, and Beauty? What have you read or heard about Wisdom, Strength and Beauty, whether inside or outside of Masonry? Simply sit for a while taking note of whatever associations arise, without concern for whether or not anything makes sense or is appropriate. If you find yourself attending to a particular association, return your focus to Wisdom, Strength, and Beauty, allowing for other associations to occur.

Pause for at least 3 minutes.

Now shift to analyzing Wisdom, Strength, and Beauty. Use your mind to carefully inspect the meanings of each word and the relationships among them. What possibilities of meaning occur to you as you do so? If some particular association grabbed your attention, you can also analyze its relationship with the words. Continue to sit in careful, penetrating examination of the focal point.

Pause for at least 3 minutes.

Now let go of your associations and analysis, and open to intuition by simply holding Wisdom, Strength, and Beauty as the focal point within the quiet, still space of your mind. Make it your intention to simply notice and release whatever arises from the mysterious depths of the psyche, allowing possibilities to come and go without trying to hold onto them or process any of them with other ways of thinking. Just keep patiently holding your attention on the focal point, gently returning your mind to the words as often as necessary.

Pause for at least 3 minutes.

For a moment now, let go of Wisdom, Strength, and Beauty, and make your focal point the quiet stillness of consciousness itself. It may help to attend to your breath, recognizing that awareness of breathing is happening within the quiet, still space of consciousness.

Pause for at least 3 minutes.

Now once again recall Wisdom, Strength, and Beauty as your focal point. Allow something from your meditation to take form as visual images and other imaginary sensations so that you can imagine somehow interacting with Wisdom, Strength, and Beauty. Let your imagination construct a kind of dream about Wisdom, Strength, and Beauty.

Pause for at least 3 minutes.

RECONNECT WITH THE PRESENT AND END THE MEDITATION

Let go of the focal point and again clear your mind as you attend to the sensations of your body. Feel gravity pulling you down into your seat and your feet against the floor. Feel the air on your skin and your breath flowing in and out. Hear what you hear. Smell what you smell and taste what you taste. When you are ready, open your eyes and see what you see.

The meditation has ended. Feel free to move and stretch your limbs.

REFLECTION

Invite participants to share their experiences, insights, and questions. Remember to use these skills:

- *welcoming sharing*

- *active listening*

- *scanning the group*

- *managing the flow*

- *being careful with advice*

WRAP UP AND CLOSE

Announce that it is time to end the session. Restate some of the more common or poignant reflections. Inform participants about the next time and location for meditation or other contemplative activities. Thank everyone for their participation.

DISCURSIVE SCRIPT #2: JACOB'S LADDER

Become thoroughly familiar with this script before using it to facilitate an activity. Notes and additional guidelines for the facilitator appear in italics, and spoken parts are indicated by a regular font. Consider your audience and what, if any, adjustments you might make in facilitating this activity. You should provide an image of Jacob's Ladder, and may wish to refresh participants' memories of the story around it. Ensure that the space is appropriately prepared.

WELCOME PARTICIPANTS

Thank everyone for coming and state it is time to focus on meditation. Ask for cell phones to be completely silenced and set an example by letting others see you doing so. Ask if you are speaking loudly enough for everyone to clearly hear you.

PROVIDE INTRODUCTIONS AS NEEDED

Unless you are certain everyone knows you, tell them your name, your connection with the fraternity, and that you will be facilitating the meditation for this session. Consider whether or not it would be helpful and time-efficient to welcome participants to introduce themselves.

EXPLAIN WHAT TO EXPECT

In this session, I am following a script from *The Contemplative Lodge: A Manual for Masons Doing Inner Work Together* we will practice discursive meditation on Jacob's Ladder. Discursive meditation consists of having a deep, contemplative discourse within yourself, using the faculties of association, analysis, intuition, and interactive imagination. I will lead you through the process of doing so. Are there any questions?

RELAXATION AND CENTERING

Closing your eyes or gazing blankly at some point in front of you, begin to relax and turn your attention inward. If you wish, take a moment to silently invoke the aid of Deity.

Pause for several breaths.

Slowly take in a deep breath, inhaling all the air you can without straining, and then hold it, hold it, hold it. Now release the breath, exhaling all the air you can without straining, and then pause, pause, pause.

Slowly take in a second deep breath, inhaling all the air you can without straining, and then hold it, hold it, hold it. Now release the breath, exhaling all the air you can without straining, and then pause, pause, pause.

Slowly take in a third deep breath, inhaling all the air you can without straining, and then hold it, hold it, hold it. Now release the breath, exhaling all the air you can without straining, and then pause, pause, pause. Now inhale and let your body breathe in its own peaceful, natural rhythm.

Pause for a couple of breaths.

Attend to the sensation of the earth's gravity pulling down on your body. Feel it pulling your feet against the floor. Feel gravity pulling down in your calves and shins. If you notice any unnecessary tension in those muscles, let it go, and let the pull of gravity take you into a deeper state of calm, peaceful relaxation.

Pause for a couple of breaths.

Feel gravity pulling down in your thighs and buttocks, pulling you into your seat. If you notice any unnecessary tension in those muscles, let it go, and let the pull of gravity take you into a deeper state of calm, peaceful relaxation.

Pause for a couple of breaths.

Feel gravity pulling down in your hips, belly, and lower back. If you notice any unnecessary tension in those muscles, let it go, leaving only what is necessary to keep you sitting in a healthy posture, and let the pull of gravity take you into a deeper state of calm, peaceful relaxation.

Pause for a couple of breaths.

Feel gravity pulling down in your ribcage, chest, and upper back. If you notice any unnecessary tension in those muscles, let it go, leaving only what is necessary to keep you sitting in a healthy posture, and let the pull of gravity take you into a deeper state of calm, peaceful relaxation.

Pause for a couple of breaths.

Feel gravity pulling down in your shoulders and neck. If you notice any unnecessary tension in those muscles, let it go, leaving only what is necessary to keep you sitting in a healthy posture, and let the pull of gravity take you into a deeper state of calm, peaceful relaxation.

Pause for a couple of breaths.

Feel gravity pulling down in your upper arms, forearms, wrists, and hands. If you notice any unnecessary tension in those muscles, let it go, and let the pull of gravity take you into a deeper state of calm, peaceful relaxation.

Pause for a couple of breaths.

Feel gravity pulling down in your jaw, your tongue, around your mouth, and in your cheeks. Feel gravity pulling down around your eyes and in your brow. Feel gravity pulling down in your scalp on the top of your head, around the sides, and down the back. If you notice any unnecessary tension in those muscles, let it go, leaving only what is necessary to keep you sitting in a healthy posture, and let the pull of gravity take you into a deeper state of calm, peaceful relaxation.

Pause for a couple of breaths.

Now, feel gravity pulling down from the top of your head all the way through every part of your body down to the soles of your feet. If you notice any unnecessary tension anywhere, let it go, leaving only what

is necessary to keep you sitting in a healthy posture, and let the pull of gravity take you into a deeper state of calm, peaceful relaxation.

Pause for a couple of breaths.

Turn your attention back to your breath, flowing in and out in its own peaceful, natural rhythm. Simply observe it flowing in and out in its own peaceful, natural rhythm. Feel each breath taking you into a deeper state of calm, peaceful relaxation.

Pause for a few breaths.

You can go into an even deeper state of calm, peaceful relaxation by silently marking the breath with the word "in" as you inhale, and "out" as you exhale: iiiiiinnn, ooouuut. Just continue observing the breath flowing in and out in its own peaceful, natural rhythm as you continue silently repeating: iiiiiinnn, ooouuut. Feel each breath taking you into a deeper state of calm, peaceful relaxation.

Pause for several breaths.

DISCURSIVE PROCESS

We now begin discursive meditation with the focal point of Jacob's Ladder. Make the title and image of Jacob's Ladder the central point within the circle of your thoughts and feelings about Jacob's Ladder. For a moment, simply sit quietly, establishing and holding that focal point within the quiet, still space of your mind.

Pause for a few breaths.

Allow your mind to make associations with the focal point. For you, what ideas, memories, or feelings naturally connect with Jacob's Ladder? What have you read or heard about Jacob's Ladder, whether inside or outside of Masonry? Simply sit for a while taking note of whatever associations arise, without concern for whether or not anything makes sense or is appropriate. If you find yourself attending to a particular association, return your focus to Jacob's Ladder, allowing for other associations to occur.

Pause for at least 3 minutes.

Now shift to analyzing Jacob's Ladder. Use your mind to carefully inspect the meanings the image, each word in the title, and the relationships among them. What possibilities of meaning occur to you as you do so? If some particular association grabbed your attention, you can also analyze its relationship with the title and image. Continue to sit in careful, penetrating examination of the focal point.

Pause for at least 3 minutes.

Now let go of your associations and analysis, and open to intuition by simply holding Jacob's Ladder as the focal point within the quiet, still space of your mind. Make it your intention to simply notice and release whatever arises from the mysterious depths of the psyche, allowing possibilities to come and go without trying to hold onto them or process any of them with other ways of thinking. Just keep patiently holding your attention on the focal point, gently returning your mind to the title and image as often as necessary.

Pause for at least 3 minutes.

For a moment now, let go of Jacob's Ladder and make your focal point the quiet stillness of consciousness itself. It may help to attend to your breath, recognizing that awareness of breathing is happening within the quiet, still space of consciousness.

Pause for at least 3 minutes.

Now once again recall Jacob's Ladder as your focal point. Allow something from your meditation to take form as visual images and other imaginary sensations so that you can imagine somehow interacting with Jacob's Ladder. Let your imagination construct a kind of dream about Jacob's Ladder.

Pause for at least 3 minutes.

RECONNECT WITH THE PRESENT AND END THE MEDITATION

Let go of the focal point and again clear your mind as you attend to the sensations of your body. Feel gravity pulling you down into your seat and your feet against the floor. Feel the air on your skin and your breath flowing in and out. Hear what you hear. Smell what you smell and taste what you taste. When you are ready, open your eyes and see what you see.

The meditation has ended. Feel free to move and stretch your limbs.

REFLECTION

Invite participants to share their experiences, insights, and questions. Remember to use these skills:

- *welcoming sharing*

- *active listening*

- *scanning the group*

- *managing the flow*

- *being careful with advice*

WRAP UP AND CLOSE

Announce that it is time to end the session. Restate some of the more common or poignant reflections. Inform participants about the next time and location for meditation or other contemplative activities. Thank everyone for their participation.

DISCURSIVE SCRIPT #3: THE MYSTIC TIE

Become thoroughly familiar with this script before using it to facilitate an activity. Notes and additional guidelines for the facilitator appear in italics, and spoken parts are indicated by a regular font. Consider your audience and what, if any, adjustments you might make in facilitating this activity. Ensure that the space is appropriately prepared.

WELCOME PARTICIPANTS

Thank everyone for coming and state it is time to focus on meditation. Ask for cell phones to be completely silenced and set an example by letting others see you doing so. Ask if you are speaking loudly enough for everyone to clearly hear you.

PROVIDE INTRODUCTIONS AS NEEDED

Unless you are certain everyone knows you, tell them your name, your connection with the fraternity, and that you will be facilitating the meditation for this session. Consider whether or not it would be helpful and time-efficient to welcome participants to introduce themselves.

EXPLAIN WHAT TO EXPECT

In this session, I am following a script from *The Contemplative Lodge: A Manual for Masons Doing Inner Work Together*, and we will practice discursive meditation on the Mystic Tie. Discursive meditation consists of having a deep, contemplative discourse within yourself, using the faculties of association, analysis, intuition, and interactive imagination. I will lead you through the process of doing so. Are there any questions?

RELAXATION AND CENTERING

Closing your eyes or gazing blankly at some point in front of you, begin to relax and turn your attention inward. If you wish, take a moment to silently invoke the aid of Deity.

Pause for several breaths.

Slowly take in a deep breath, inhaling all the air you can without straining, and then hold it, hold it, hold it. Now release the breath, exhaling all the air you can without straining, and then pause, pause, pause.

Slowly take in a second deep breath, inhaling all the air you can without straining, and then hold it, hold it, hold it. Now release the breath, exhaling all the air you can without straining, and then pause, pause, pause.

Slowly take in a third deep breath, inhaling all the air you can without straining, and then hold it, hold it, hold it. Now release the breath, exhaling all the air you can without straining, and then pause, pause, pause. Now inhale and let your body breathe in its own peaceful, natural rhythm.

Pause for a couple of breaths.

Attend to the sensation of the earth's gravity pulling down on your body. Feel it pulling your feet against the floor. Feel gravity pulling down in your calves and shins. If you notice any unnecessary tension in those muscles, let it go, and let the pull of gravity take you into a deeper state of calm, peaceful relaxation.

Pause for a couple of breaths.

Feel gravity pulling down in your thighs and buttocks, pulling you into your seat. If you notice any unnecessary tension in those muscles, let it go, and let the pull of gravity take you into a deeper state of calm, peaceful relaxation.

Pause for a couple of breaths.

Feel gravity pulling down in your hips, belly, and lower back. If you notice any unnecessary tension in those muscles, let it go, leaving only what is necessary to keep you sitting in a healthy posture, and let the pull of gravity take you into a deeper state of calm, peaceful relaxation.

Pause for a couple of breaths.

Feel gravity pulling down in your ribcage, chest, and upper back. If you notice any unnecessary tension in those muscles, let it go, leaving only what is necessary to keep you sitting in a healthy posture, and let the pull of gravity take you into a deeper state of calm, peaceful relaxation.

Pause for a couple of breaths.

Feel gravity pulling down in your shoulders and neck. If you notice any unnecessary tension in those muscles, let it go, leaving only what

is necessary to keep you sitting in a healthy posture, and let the pull of gravity take you into a deeper state of calm, peaceful relaxation.

Pause for a couple of breaths.

Feel gravity pulling down in your upper arms, forearms, wrists, and hands. If you notice any unnecessary tension in those muscles, let it go, and let the pull of gravity take you into a deeper state of calm, peaceful relaxation.

Pause for a couple of breaths.

Feel gravity pulling down in your jaw, your tongue, around your mouth, and in your cheeks. Feel gravity pulling down around your eyes and in your brow. Feel gravity pulling down in your scalp on the top of your head, around the sides, and down the back. If you notice any unnecessary tension in those muscles, let it go, leaving only what is necessary to keep you sitting in a healthy posture, and let the pull of gravity take you into a deeper state of calm, peaceful relaxation.

Pause for a couple of breaths.

Now, feel gravity pulling down from the top of your head all the way through every part of your body down to the soles of your feet. If you notice any unnecessary tension anywhere, let it go, leaving only what

is necessary to keep you sitting in a healthy posture, and let the pull of gravity take you into a deeper state of calm, peaceful relaxation.

Pause for a couple of breaths.

Turn your attention back to your breath, flowing in and out in its own peaceful, natural rhythm. Simply observe it flowing in and out in its own peaceful, natural rhythm. Feel each breath taking you into a deeper state of calm, peaceful relaxation.

Pause for a few breaths.

You can go into an even deeper state of calm, peaceful relaxation by silently marking the breath with the word "in" as you inhale, and "out" as you exhale: iiiiiinnn, ooouuut. Just continue observing the breath flowing in and out in its own peaceful, natural rhythm as you continue silently repeating: iiiiiinnn, ooouuut. Feel each breath taking you into a deeper state of calm, peaceful relaxation.

Pause for several breaths.

Discursive Process

We now begin discursive meditation with the focal point of the Mystic Tie. Make the words, Mystic Tie, the central point within the circle of your thoughts and feelings about the Mystic Tie. For a moment, simply sit quietly, establishing and holding that focal point within the quiet, still space of your mind.

Pause for a few breaths.

Allow your mind to make associations with the focal point. For you, what ideas, memories, or feelings naturally connect with the Mystic Tie? What have you read or heard about the Mystic Tie, whether inside or outside of Masonry? Simply sit for a while taking note of whatever associations arise, without concern for whether or not anything makes sense or is appropriate. If you find yourself attending to a particular association, return your focus to the Mystic Tie, allowing for other associations to occur.

Pause for at least 3 minutes.

Now shift to analyzing the Mystic Tie. Use your mind to carefully inspect the meanings of each word and the relationships among them. What possibilities of meaning occur to you as you do so? If some particular association grabbed your attention, you can also analyze its relationship with the words. Continue to sit in careful, penetrating examination of the focal point.

Pause for at least 3 minutes.

Now let go of your associations and analysis, and open to intuition by simply holding the Mystic Tie as the focal point within the quiet, still space of your mind. Make it your intention to simply notice and release whatever arises from the mysterious depths of the psyche, allowing possibilities to come and go without trying to hold onto them or process any of them with other ways of thinking. Just keep patiently holding your attention on the focal point, gently returning your mind to the words, Mystic Tie, as often as necessary.

Pause for at least 3 minutes.

For a moment now, let go of the Mystic Tie and make your focal point the quiet stillness of consciousness itself. It may help to attend to your breath, recognizing that awareness of breathing is happening within the quiet, still space of consciousness.

Pause for at least 3 minutes.

Now once again recall the Mystic Tie as your focal point. Allow something from your meditation to take form as visual images and other imaginary sensations so that you can imagine somehow interacting with the Mystic Tie. Let your imagination construct a kind of dream about the Mystic Tie.

Pause for at least 3 minutes.

RECONNECT WITH THE PRESENT AND END THE MEDITATION

Let go of the focal point and again clear your mind as you attend to the sensations of your body. Feel gravity pulling you down into your seat and your feet against the floor. Feel the air on your skin and your breath flowing in and out. Hear what you hear. Smell what you smell and taste what you taste. When you are ready, open your eyes and see what you see.

The meditation has ended. Feel free to move and stretch your limbs.

REFLECTION

Invite participants to share their experiences, insights, and questions. Remember to use these skills:

- *welcoming sharing*
- *active listening*
- *scanning the group*
- *managing the flow*
- *being careful with advice*

WRAP UP AND CLOSE

Announce that it is time to end the session. Restate some of the more common or poignant reflections. Inform participants about the next time and location for meditation or other contemplative activities. Thank everyone for their participation.

CHANTING SCRIPT #1: AMEN

Become thoroughly familiar with this script before using it to facilitate an activity. Notes and additional guidelines for the facilitator appear in italics, and spoken parts are indicated by a regular font. Consider your audience and what, if any, adjustments you might make in facilitating this activity. Ensure that the space is appropriately prepared.

WELCOME PARTICIPANTS

Thank everyone for coming and state it is time to focus on meditation. Ask for cell phones to be completely silenced and set an example by letting others see you doing so. Ask if you are speaking loudly enough for everyone to clearly hear you.

PROVIDE INTRODUCTIONS AS NEEDED

Unless you are certain everyone knows you, tell them your name, your connection with the fraternity, and that you will be facilitating the meditation for this session. Consider whether or not it would be helpful and time-efficient to welcome participants to introduce themselves.

EXPLAIN WHAT TO EXPECT

In this meditation we will be chanting *amen* (ah-men), and I am following a script from *The Contemplative Lodge: A Manual for Masons Doing Inner Work Together.* This is the Hebrew word for "so mote it be," which has obvious ritual significance to Masons of all degrees. However, there are depths of meaning that go far beyond the ritualistic ending of a prayer. It is a plea to let something be so, an affirmation that it will be so, and also a declaration of acceptance about what is. Due to the great familiarity most people have with it, amen is perhaps the very best way to introduce the power of chanting. As we perform this chant, we will intone amen by stretching out all its sounds through a complete exhalation, like this: aaammmeeennn.

As we chant the word, focus your awareness on the sensations in your body, on where and how you feel the vibrations, and on any emotions it might stir. The object is to feel the sounds more than think about their meaning. We will chant aloud several times and then switch to a silent, internal chant, keeping the same pace of our breath and imagining the sounds of the word flowing through us with each exhalation. After several silent repetitions, we will stop the chant and sit in silence for a while before ending the meditation. Are there any questions?

RELAXATION AND CENTERING

Closing your eyes or gazing blankly at some point in front of you, begin to relax and turn your attention inward. If you wish, take a moment to silently invoke the aid of Deity.

Pause for several breaths.

Slowly take in a deep breath, inhaling all the air you can without straining, and then hold it, hold it, hold it. Now release the breath, exhaling all the air you can without straining, and then pause, pause, pause.

Slowly take in a second deep breath, inhaling all the air you can without straining, and then hold it, hold it, hold it. Now release the breath, exhaling all the air you can without straining, and then pause, pause, pause.

Slowly take in a third deep breath, inhaling all the air you can without straining, and then hold it, hold it, hold it. Now release the breath, exhaling all the air you can without straining, and then pause, pause, pause. Now inhale and let your body breathe in its own peaceful, natural rhythm.

Pause for a couple of breaths.

Attend to the sensation of the earth's gravity pulling down on your body. Feel it pulling your feet against the floor. Feel gravity pulling down in your calves and shins. If you notice any unnecessary tension in those muscles, let it go, and let the pull of gravity take you into a deeper state of calm, peaceful relaxation.

Pause for a couple of breaths.

Feel gravity pulling down in your thighs and buttocks, pulling you into your seat. If you notice any unnecessary tension in those muscles, let it go, and let the pull of gravity take you into a deeper state of calm, peaceful relaxation.

Pause for a couple of breaths.

Feel gravity pulling down in your hips, belly, and lower back. If you notice any unnecessary tension in those muscles, let it go, leaving only what is necessary to keep you sitting in a healthy posture, and

let the pull of gravity take you into a deeper state of calm, peaceful relaxation.

Pause for a couple of breaths.

Feel gravity pulling down in your ribcage, chest, and upper back. If you notice any unnecessary tension in those muscles, let it go, leaving only what is necessary to keep you sitting in a healthy posture, and let the pull of gravity take you into a deeper state of calm, peaceful relaxation.

Pause for a couple of breaths.

Feel gravity pulling down in your shoulders and neck. If you notice any unnecessary tension in those muscles, let it go, leaving only what is necessary to keep you sitting in a healthy posture, and let the pull of gravity take you into a deeper state of calm, peaceful relaxation.

Pause for a couple of breaths.

Feel gravity pulling down in your upper arms, forearms, wrists, and hands. If you notice any unnecessary tension in those muscles, let it go, and let the pull of gravity take you into a deeper state of calm, peaceful relaxation.

Pause for a couple of breaths.

Feel gravity pulling down in your jaw, your tongue, around your mouth, and in your cheeks. Feel gravity pulling down around your eyes and in your brow. Feel gravity pulling down in your scalp on the top of your head, around the sides, and down the back. If you notice any unnecessary tension in those muscles, let it go, leaving only what is necessary to keep you sitting in a healthy posture, and let the pull of gravity take you into a deeper state of calm, peaceful relaxation.

Pause for a couple of breaths.

Now, feel gravity pulling down from the top of your head all the way through every part of your body down to the soles of your feet. If you notice any unnecessary tension anywhere, let it go, leaving only what is necessary to keep you sitting in a healthy posture, and let the pull of gravity take you into a deeper state of calm, peaceful relaxation.

Pause for a couple of breaths.

Turn your attention back to your breath, flowing in and out in its own peaceful, natural rhythm. Simply observe it flowing in and out in its own peaceful, natural rhythm. Feel each breath taking you into a deeper state of calm, peaceful relaxation.

Pause for a few breaths.

You can go into an even deeper state of calm, peaceful relaxation by silently marking the breath with the word "in" as you inhale, and "out" as you exhale: iiiiiinnn, ooouuut. Just continue observing the breath flowing in and out in its own peaceful, natural rhythm as you continue silently repeating: iiiiiinnn, ooouuut. Feel each breath taking you into a deeper state of calm, peaceful relaxation.

Pause for several breaths.

INTONING THE CHANT

Let go of marking the breath with the words in and out. We are about to chant amen, moving gradually through the sounds of the word as it stretches out through each exhalation. As we chant, pay attention to feeling the vibrations and how they change with the specific sounds of the letters. Note the effects of the chant on your mind, body, and emotions.

Begin the chant and continue through at least 10 repetitions.

Now rest, and we will switch to a silent, internal chant, keeping the same pace of our breath and imagining the sounds of the word flowing through us with each exhalation.

Pause for at least 10 repetitions.

Now rest. Let go of the chant and sit in silence for a while, attending to any effects from the chant on your mind, body, and emotions.

Pause for at least 3 minutes.

Now once again focus upon the breath flowing in and out in its own peaceful, natural rhythm.

Pause for a few breaths.

RECONNECT WITH THE PRESENT AND END THE MEDITATION

Attend to the sensations of your body. Feel gravity pulling you down into your seat and your feet against the floor. Feel the air on your skin and your breath flowing in and out. Hear what you hear. Smell what you smell and taste what you taste. When you are ready, open your eyes and see what you see.

The meditation has ended. Feel free to move and stretch your limbs.

REFLECTION

Invite participants to share their experiences, insights, and questions. Remember to use these skills:

- *welcoming sharing*
- *active listening*
- *scanning the group*
- *managing the flow*
- *being careful with advice*

WRAP UP AND CLOSE

Announce that it is time to end the session. Restate some of the more common or poignant reflections. Inform participants about the next time and location for meditation or other contemplative activities. Thank everyone for their participation.

CHANTING SCRIPT #2: HARMONIA

Become thoroughly familiar with this script before using it to facilitate an activity. Notes and additional guidelines for the facilitator appear in italics, and spoken parts are indicated by a regular font. Consider your audience and what, if any, adjustments you might make in facilitating this activity. Ensure that the space is appropriately prepared.

WELCOME PARTICIPANTS

Thank everyone for coming and state it is time to focus on meditation. Ask for cell phones to be completely silenced and set an example by letting others see you doing so. Ask if you are speaking loudly enough for everyone to clearly hear you.

PROVIDE INTRODUCTIONS AS NEEDED

Unless you are certain everyone knows you, tell them your name, your connection with the fraternity, and that you will be facilitating the meditation for this session. Consider whether or not it would be helpful and time-efficient to welcome participants to introduce themselves.

EXPLAIN WHAT TO EXPECT

Our tradition refers to peace and harmony as the chief strength of all well-regulated institutions, more especially this of ours. In this meditation we will therefore be chanting *harmonia* (har-MOH-nee-ah), and I am following a script from *The Contemplative Lodge: A Manual for Masons Doing Inner Work Together*. This is a Greek word meaning an agreement or concord of sounds; it is also the name of the Greek goddess of music.[35] The word originally literally referred to a means of joining – such as with the planks of a ship – and was also used with regard to a settled government or order. It thus signifies the parts of something being properly and securely joined in a well-functioning and pleasing manner. As we perform this chant, we will intone "harmonia" by stretching out all its sounds through a complete exhalation, like this: hhhaaarrrmmmooonnniiiaaa.

As we chant the word, focus your awareness on the sensations in your body, on where and how you feel the vibrations, and on any emotions it might stir. The object is to feel the sounds more than think about their meaning. We will chant aloud several times and then switch to a silent, internal chant, keeping the same pace of our breath and imagining the sounds of the word flowing through us with each exhalation. After several silent repetitions, we will stop the chant and sit in silence for a while before ending the meditation. Are there any questions?

RELAXATION AND CENTERING

Closing your eyes or gazing blankly at some point in front of you, begin to relax and turn your attention inward. If you wish, take a moment to silently invoke the aid of Deity.

Pause for several breaths.

---

35. *Online Etymology Dictionary*, https://www.etymonline.com/word/harmony, accessed 2019.

Slowly take in a deep breath, inhaling all the air you can without straining, and then hold it, hold it, hold it. Now release the breath, exhaling all the air you can without straining, and then pause, pause, pause.

Slowly take in a second deep breath, inhaling all the air you can without straining, and then hold it, hold it, hold it. Now release the breath, exhaling all the air you can without straining, and then pause, pause, pause.

Slowly take in a third deep breath, inhaling all the air you can without straining, and then hold it, hold it, hold it. Now release the breath, exhaling all the air you can without straining, and then pause, pause, pause. Now inhale and let your body breathe in its own peaceful, natural rhythm.

Pause for a couple of breaths.

Attend to the sensation of the earth's gravity pulling down on your body. Feel it pulling your feet against the floor. Feel gravity pulling down in your calves and shins. If you notice any unnecessary tension in those muscles, let it go, and let the pull of gravity take you into a deeper state of calm, peaceful relaxation.

Pause for a couple of breaths.

Feel gravity pulling down in your thighs and buttocks, pulling you into your seat. If you notice any unnecessary tension in those muscles, let it go, and let the pull of gravity take you into a deeper state of calm, peaceful relaxation.

Pause for a couple of breaths.

Feel gravity pulling down in your hips, belly, and lower back. If you notice any unnecessary tension in those muscles, let it go, leaving only what is necessary to keep you sitting in a healthy posture, and let the pull of gravity take you into a deeper state of calm, peaceful relaxation.

Pause for a couple of breaths.

Feel gravity pulling down in your ribcage, chest, and upper back. If you notice any unnecessary tension in those muscles, let it go, leaving only what is necessary to keep you sitting in a healthy posture, and let the pull of gravity take you into a deeper state of calm, peaceful relaxation.

Pause for a couple of breaths.

Feel gravity pulling down in your shoulders and neck. If you notice any unnecessary tension in those muscles, let it go, leaving only what is necessary to keep you sitting in a healthy posture, and let the pull of gravity take you into a deeper state of calm, peaceful relaxation.

Pause for a couple of breaths.

Feel gravity pulling down in your upper arms, forearms, wrists, and hands. If you notice any unnecessary tension in those muscles, let it go, and let the pull of gravity take you into a deeper state of calm, peaceful relaxation.

Pause for a couple of breaths.

Feel gravity pulling down in your jaw, your tongue, around your mouth, and in your cheeks. Feel gravity pulling down around your eyes and in your brow. Feel gravity pulling down in your scalp on the top of your head, around the sides, and down the back. If you notice any unnecessary tension in those muscles, let it go, leaving only what is necessary to keep you sitting in a healthy posture, and let the pull of gravity take you into a deeper state of calm, peaceful relaxation.

Pause for a couple of breaths.

Now, feel gravity pulling down from the top of your head all the way through every part of your body down to the soles of your feet. If you notice any unnecessary tension anywhere, let it go, leaving only what is necessary to keep you sitting in a healthy posture, and let the pull of gravity take you into a deeper state of calm, peaceful relaxation.

Pause for a couple of breaths.

Turn your attention back to your breath, flowing in and out in its own peaceful, natural rhythm. Simply observe it flowing in and out in its own peaceful, natural rhythm. Feel each breath taking you into a deeper state of calm, peaceful relaxation.

Pause for a few breaths.

You can go into an even deeper state of calm, peaceful relaxation by silently marking the breath with the word "in" as you inhale, and "out" as you exhale: iiiiiinnn, ooouuut. Just continue observing the breath flowing in and out in its own peaceful, natural rhythm as you continue silently repeating: iiiiiinnn, ooouuut. Feel each breath taking you into a deeper state of calm, peaceful relaxation.

Pause for several breaths.

INTONING THE CHANT

Let go of marking the breath with the words in and out. We are about to chant "harmonia," moving gradually through the sounds of the word as it stretches out through each exhalation. As we chant, pay attention to feeling the vibrations and how they change with the specific sounds of the letters. Note the effects of the chant on your mind, body, and emotions.

Begin the chant and continue through at least 10 repetitions.

Now rest, and we will switch to a silent, internal chant, keeping the same pace of our breath and imagining the sounds of the word flowing through us with each exhalation.

Pause for at least 10 repetitions.

Now rest. Let go of the chant and sit in silence for a while, attending to any effects from the chant on your mind, body, and emotions.

Pause for at least 3 minutes.

Now once again focus upon the breath flowing in and out in its own peaceful, natural rhythm.

Pause for a few breaths.

RECONNECT WITH THE PRESENT AND END THE MEDITATION

Attend to the sensations of your body. Feel gravity pulling you down into your seat and your feet against the floor. Feel the air on your skin and your breath flowing in and out. Hear what you hear. Smell what you smell and taste what you taste. When you are ready, open your eyes and see what you see.

The meditation has ended. Feel free to move and stretch your limbs.

REFLECTION

Invite participants to share their experiences, insights, and questions. Remember to use these skills:

- *welcoming sharing*
- *active listening*
- *scanning the group*
- *managing the flow*
- *being careful with advice*

WRAP UP AND CLOSE

Announce that it is time to end the session. Restate some of the more common or poignant reflections. Inform participants about the next time and location for meditation or other contemplative activities. Thank everyone for their participation.

CHANTING SCRIPT #3: CARITAS

Become thoroughly familiar with this script before using it to facilitate an activity. Notes and additional guidelines for the facilitator appear in italics, and spoken parts are indicated by a regular font. Consider your audience and what, if any, adjustments you might make in facilitating this activity. Ensure that the space is appropriately prepared.

WELCOME PARTICIPANTS

Thank everyone for coming and state it is time to focus on meditation. Ask for cell phones to be completely silenced and set an example by letting others see you doing so. Ask if you are speaking loudly enough for everyone to clearly hear you.

PROVIDE INTRODUCTIONS AS NEEDED

Unless you are certain everyone knows you, tell them your name, your connection with the fraternity, and that you will be facilitating the meditation for this session. Consider whether or not it would be helpful and time-efficient to welcome participants to introduce themselves.

EXPLAIN WHAT TO EXPECT

In this meditation we will be chanting *caritas* (KAH-ree-tahs), and I am following a script from *The Contemplative Lodge: A Manual for Masons Doing Inner Work Together*. Caritas is a Latin word for love used in the original description of the Three Theological Virtues found in the New Testament, First Corinthians, Chapter 13, and was

often translated into the English word *charity*. As a theological virtue, caritas refers to compassionate, merciful, unconditional care and
concern for others, and also has relevance to many other teachings
about love in Masonry.[36] As we perform this chant, we will intone
"caritas" by stretching out all its sounds through a complete exhalation, like this: kaaarrreeetaaasss.

As we chant the word, focus your awareness on the sensations in your
body, on where and how you feel the vibrations, and on any emotions it might stir. The object is to feel the sounds more than think
about their meaning. We will chant aloud several times and then
switch to a silent, internal chant, keeping the same pace of our breath
and imagining the sounds of the word flowing through us with each
exhalation. After several silent repetitions, we will stop the chant and
sit in silence for a while before ending the meditation. Are there any
questions?

RELAXATION AND CENTERING

Closing your eyes or gazing blankly at some point in front of you,
begin to relax and turn your attention inward. If you wish, take a
moment to silently invoke the aid of Deity.

Pause for several breaths.

Slowly take in a deep breath, inhaling all the air you can without
straining, and then hold it, hold it, hold it. Now release the breath,

36. *Online Etymology Dictionary*, https://www.etymonline.com/word/charity,
accessed 2019.

exhaling all the air you can without straining, and then pause, pause, pause.

Slowly take in a second deep breath, inhaling all the air you can without straining, and then hold it, hold it, hold it. Now release the breath, exhaling all the air you can without straining, and then pause, pause, pause.

Slowly take in a third deep breath, inhaling all the air you can without straining, and then hold it, hold it, hold it. Now release the breath, exhaling all the air you can without straining, and then pause, pause, pause. Now inhale and let your body breathe in its own peaceful, natural rhythm.

Pause for a couple of breaths.

Attend to the sensation of the earth's gravity pulling down on your body. Feel it pulling your feet against the floor. Feel gravity pulling down in your calves and shins. If you notice any unnecessary tension in those muscles, let it go, and let the pull of gravity take you into a deeper state of calm, peaceful relaxation.

Pause for a couple of breaths.

Feel gravity pulling down in your thighs and buttocks, pulling you into your seat. If you notice any unnecessary tension in those muscles, let it go, and let the pull of gravity take you into a deeper state of calm, peaceful relaxation.

Pause for a couple of breaths.

Feel gravity pulling down in your hips, belly, and lower back. If you notice any unnecessary tension in those muscles, let it go, leaving only what is necessary to keep you sitting in a healthy posture, and let the pull of gravity take you into a deeper state of calm, peaceful relaxation.

Pause for a couple of breaths.

Feel gravity pulling down in your ribcage, chest, and upper back. If you notice any unnecessary tension in those muscles, let it go, leaving only what is necessary to keep you sitting in a healthy posture, and let the pull of gravity take you into a deeper state of calm, peaceful relaxation.

Pause for a couple of breaths.

Feel gravity pulling down in your shoulders and neck. If you notice any unnecessary tension in those muscles, let it go, leaving only what is necessary to keep you sitting in a healthy posture, and let the pull of gravity take you into a deeper state of calm, peaceful relaxation.

Pause for a couple of breaths.

Feel gravity pulling down in your upper arms, forearms, wrists, and hands. If you notice any unnecessary tension in those muscles, let it go, and let the pull of gravity take you into a deeper state of calm, peaceful relaxation.

Pause for a couple of breaths.

Feel gravity pulling down in your jaw, your tongue, around your mouth, and in your cheeks. Feel gravity pulling down around your eyes and in your brow. Feel gravity pulling down in your scalp on the top of your head, around the sides, and down the back. If you notice any unnecessary tension in those muscles, let it go, leaving only what is necessary to keep you sitting in a healthy posture, and let the pull of gravity take you into a deeper state of calm, peaceful relaxation.

Pause for a couple of breaths.

Now, feel gravity pulling down from the top of your head all the way through every part of your body down to the soles of your feet. If you notice any unnecessary tension anywhere, let it go, leaving only what is necessary to keep you sitting in a healthy posture, and let the pull of gravity take you into a deeper state of calm, peaceful relaxation.

Pause for a couple of breaths.

Turn your attention back to your breath, flowing in and out in its own peaceful, natural rhythm. Simply observe it flowing in and out in its own peaceful, natural rhythm. Feel each breath taking you into a deeper state of calm, peaceful relaxation.

Pause for a few breaths.

You can go into an even deeper state of calm, peaceful relaxation by silently marking the breath with the word "in" as you inhale, and "out" as you exhale: iiiiiinnn, ooouuut. Just continue observing the breath flowing in and out in its own peaceful, natural rhythm as you continue silently repeating: iiiiiinnn, ooouuut. Feel each breath taking you into a deeper state of calm, peaceful relaxation.

Pause for several breaths.

INTONING THE CHANT

Let go of marking the breath with the words in and out. We are about to chant "caritas," moving gradually through the sounds of the word as it stretches out through each exhalation. As we chant, pay attention to feeling the vibrations and how they change with the specific sounds of the letters. Note the effects of the chant on your mind, body, and emotions.

Begin the chant and continue through at least 10 repetitions.

Now rest, and we will switch to a silent, internal chant, keeping the same pace of our breath and imagining the sounds of the word flowing through us with each exhalation.

Pause for at least 10 repetitions.

Now rest. Let go of the chant and sit in silence for a while, attending to any effects from the chant on your mind, body, and emotions.

Pause for at least 3 minutes.

Now once again focus upon the breath flowing in and out in its own peaceful, natural rhythm.

Pause for a few breaths.

RECONNECT WITH THE PRESENT AND END THE MEDITATION

Attend to the sensations of your body. Feel gravity pulling you down into your seat and your feet against the floor. Feel the air on your skin and your breath flowing in and out. Hear what you hear. Smell what you smell and taste what you taste. When you are ready, open your eyes and see what you see.

The meditation has ended. Feel free to move and stretch your limbs.

REFLECTION

Invite participants to share their experiences, insights, and questions. Remember to use these skills:

- *welcoming sharing*

- *active listening*

- *scanning the group*

- *managing the flow*

- *being careful with advice*

WRAP UP AND CLOSE

Announce that it is time to end the session. Restate some of the more common or poignant reflections. Inform participants about the next time and location for meditation or other contemplative activities. Thank everyone for their participation.

GUIDED IMAGERY SCRIPT #1: VISITING A LODGE ROOM

Become thoroughly familiar with this script before using it to facilitate an activity. Notes and additional guidelines for the facilitator appear in italics, and spoken parts are indicated by a regular font. Consider your audience and what, if any, adjustments you might make in facilitating this activity. Ensure that the space is appropriately prepared.

WELCOME PARTICIPANTS

Thank everyone for coming and state it is time to focus on meditation. Ask for cell phones to be completely silenced and set an example by letting others see you doing so. Ask if you are speaking loudly enough for everyone to clearly hear you.

PROVIDE INTRODUCTIONS AS NEEDED

Unless you are certain everyone knows you, tell them your name, your connection with the fraternity, and that you will be facilitating the meditation for this session. Consider whether or not it would be helpful and time-efficient to welcome participants to introduce themselves.

EXPLAIN WHAT TO EXPECT

In this session, I am following a script from *The Contemplative Lodge: A Manual for Masons Doing Inner Work Together*, and we will practice a guided imagery meditation on visiting a lodge room. I will provide structure and detail while leading you through an extended imaginary experience. In effect, you will participate in a story I am telling. Unless I say otherwise, imagine only what I describe, and if other images come up, simply return your attention to imagining what I describe as vividly as possible. This type of meditation intentionally involves complex symbolism with which you can interact to develop your own insights and questions for further contemplation. Are there any questions?

RELAXATION AND CENTERING

Closing your eyes or gazing blankly at some point in front of you, begin to relax and turn your attention inward. If you wish, take a moment to silently invoke the aid of Deity.

Pause for several breaths.

Slowly take in a deep breath, inhaling all the air you can without straining, and then hold it, hold it, hold it. Now release the breath, exhaling all the air you can without straining, and then pause, pause, pause.

Slowly take in a second deep breath, inhaling all the air you can without straining, and then hold it, hold it, hold it. Now release the breath, exhaling all the air you can without straining, and then pause, pause, pause.

Slowly take in a third deep breath, inhaling all the air you can without straining, and then hold it, hold it, hold it. Now release the breath, exhaling all the air you can without straining, and then pause, pause,

pause. Now inhale and let your body breathe in its own peaceful, natural rhythm.

Pause for a couple of breaths.

Attend to the sensation of the earth's gravity pulling down on your body. Feel it pulling your feet against the floor. Feel gravity pulling down in your calves and shins. If you notice any unnecessary tension in those muscles, let it go, and let the pull of gravity take you into a deeper state of calm, peaceful relaxation.

Pause for a couple of breaths.

Feel gravity pulling down in your thighs and buttocks, pulling you into your seat. If you notice any unnecessary tension in those muscles, let it go, and let the pull of gravity take you into a deeper state of calm, peaceful relaxation.

Pause for a couple of breaths.

Feel gravity pulling down in your hips, belly, and lower back. If you notice any unnecessary tension in those muscles, let it go, leaving only what is necessary to keep you sitting in a healthy posture, and let the pull of gravity take you into a deeper state of calm, peaceful relaxation.

Pause for a couple of breaths.

Feel gravity pulling down in your ribcage, chest, and upper back. If you notice any unnecessary tension in those muscles, let it go, leaving only what is necessary to keep you sitting in a healthy posture, and

let the pull of gravity take you into a deeper state of calm, peaceful relaxation.

Pause for a couple of breaths.

Feel gravity pulling down in your shoulders and neck. If you notice any unnecessary tension in those muscles, let it go, leaving only what is necessary to keep you sitting in a healthy posture, and let the pull of gravity take you into a deeper state of calm, peaceful relaxation.

Pause for a couple of breaths.

Feel gravity pulling down in your upper arms, forearms, wrists, and hands. If you notice any unnecessary tension in those muscles, let it go, and let the pull of gravity take you into a deeper state of calm, peaceful relaxation.

Pause for a couple of breaths.

Feel gravity pulling down in your jaw, your tongue, around your mouth, and in your cheeks. Feel gravity pulling down around your eyes and in your brow. Feel gravity pulling down in your scalp on the top of your head, around the sides, and down the back. If you notice any unnecessary tension in those muscles, let it go, leaving only what is necessary to keep you sitting in a healthy posture, and let the pull of gravity take you into a deeper state of calm, peaceful relaxation.

Pause for a couple of breaths.

Now, feel gravity pulling down from the top of your head all the way through every part of your body down to the soles of your feet. If you notice any unnecessary tension anywhere, let it go, leaving only what is necessary to keep you sitting in a healthy posture, and let the pull of gravity take you into a deeper state of calm, peaceful relaxation.

Pause for a couple of breaths.

Turn your attention back to your breath, flowing in and out in its own peaceful, natural rhythm. Simply observe it flowing in and out in its own peaceful, natural rhythm. Feel each breath taking you into a deeper state of calm, peaceful relaxation.

Pause for a few breaths.

You can go into an even deeper state of calm, peaceful relaxation by silently marking the breath with the word "in" as you inhale, and "out" as you exhale: iiiiiinnn, ooouuut. Just continue observing the breath flowing in and out in its own peaceful, natural rhythm as you continue silently repeating: iiiiiinnn, ooouuut. Feel each breath taking you into a deeper state of calm, peaceful relaxation.

Pause for several breaths.

IMAGERY PROCESS

Now imagine yourself standing outside the open door of an empty lodge room, one that you are very familiar with. Remaining outside the lodge room, you look inside and see it is prepared for work, with the Three Great Lights on the altar, the Three Tapers near the altar, and everything else in place. Try to see as much detail as possible without getting too focused on any single thing. Take note of the lighting, colors, smell, and quietness of the room.

Pause for a few breaths.

In your hands you have a plain, white lambskin apron. Look at the apron in your hands. See all of its details, such as its seams. Feel its weight, textures, and edges. Smell it. Recall what our tradition says about this badge and emblem of a Mason.

Pause for a few breaths.

Look down and see yourself dressed in the way you believe is most appropriate for this moment. Notice some of the details of your clothing.

Pause for a few breaths.

Begin slowly going through the process of putting on your apron. Take it step by step, mindfully experiencing every aspect, seeing it and feeling it as clearly as possible without becoming too focused on any particular detail.

Pause for a few breaths.

Now stand erect, properly clothed and mindful that you are about to cross the threshold from the profane world into the sacred space of the lodge room. As you stand there, fill your heart and mind with the appropriate attitude for entering this space, with centuries of tradition built into its form, furnishings, and decorations.

Pause for a few breaths.

With your left foot first, step across the threshold, and feel yourself passing through it, as if stepping through an invisible veil that sweeps through your body, mind, and soul, so that you stand just inside the door of the lodge room, mindful that you have left the profane world behind. Feel the energy of the atmosphere. Try to describe that energy to yourself.

Pause for a few breaths.

Begin walking toward the altar, observing the North of the lodge room. Then with mindfulness in each movement, slowly approach the altar in the manner you learned for the highest Blue Lodge degree you have received. Recall what you were taught about the symbolism of those movements.

Pause for a few breaths.

Remaining at the altar, look toward the Master's station in the East. Observe all the furnishings, implements, and decorations, recalling their traditional meanings.

Pause for a few breaths.

Remaining at the altar, turn to your right and look toward the Junior Warden's station in the South. Observe all the furnishings, implements, and decorations, recalling their traditional meanings.

Pause for a few breaths.

Remaining at the altar, turn to your right and look toward the Senior Warden's station in the West. Observe all the furnishings, implements, and decorations, recalling their traditional meanings.

Pause for a few breaths.

Remaining at the altar, turn to your right and again look toward the East. Now direct your attention to the Secretary's desk and see that there is a single white envelope and a pen lying on top. Leave the altar and mindfully walk to the Secretary's desk.

Pause for a few breaths.

Look at the pen and envelope on the Secretary's desk and see that the envelope has your name written on it. This envelope has been left for you, so mindfully reach to pick it up. See and feel your hand picking up the envelope. Feel its light weight, its texture, and edges. See all of its details.

Pause for a few breaths.

Be aware that the envelope and its contents have been left as a source of Masonic light for you and slowly open the envelope – seeing, feeling, and hearing every step in the process – to discover that there is a folded piece of paper inside.

See and feel your hands taking out the piece of paper and unfolding it to find something that has been written or drawn on it for you. Whatever you first see, no matter what it is, accept it and try to see it as clearly as possible.

Pause for a few breaths.

For a moment now, contemplate the light you have just received.

Pause for a few breaths.

Now put the envelope and paper on the desk, mindfully pick up the pen, and write and sign a short note of thanks on the paper.

Pause for a few breaths.

Pick up the paper, carefully fold it, and return it to the envelope. Place the envelope back on the Secretary's desk. Then mindfully return to the west side of the altar.

Pause for several breaths.

Once again approach the altar in the manner of your highest Blue Lodge degree and, once that process has been completed, walk back to stand just inside the open door of the lodge room, looking out.

Pause for a few breaths.

Be aware that you are about to cross the threshold from the sacred space of the lodge room into the profane world. With your left foot first, step across the threshold and feel yourself passing through it, as if stepping through an invisible veil that sweeps through your body, mind, and soul, so that you stand just outside the door of the lodge room, mindful that you have returned to the profane world bringing with you some of the energy of the lodge room as well as the light you received from the envelope on the Secretary's desk.

Pause for a few breaths.

Look down, see your clothing and white lambskin apron, and carefully see and feel your hands removing the apron.

Pause for a few breaths.

RECONNECT WITH THE PRESENT AND END THE MEDITATION

Release the imagery and again clear your mind as you attend to the sensations of your body right here. Feel gravity pulling you down into your seat and your feet against the floor. Feel the air on your skin and your breath flowing in and out. Hear what you hear. Smell what you smell and taste what you taste. When you are ready, open your eyes and see what you see.

The meditation has ended. Feel free to move and stretch your limbs.

REFLECTION

Invite participants to share their experiences, insights, and questions. Remember to use these skills:

- *welcoming sharing*

- *active listening*

- *scanning the group*

- *managing the flow*

- *being careful with advice*

WRAP UP AND CLOSE

Announce that it is time to end the session. Restate some of the more common or poignant reflections. Inform participants about the next time and location for meditation or other contemplative activities. Thank everyone for their participation.

Guided Imagery Script #2: Working in the Quarry

Become thoroughly familiar with this script before using it to facilitate an activity. Notes and additional guidelines for the facilitator appear in italics, and spoken parts are indicated by a regular font. Consider your audience and what, if any, adjustments you might make in facilitating this activity. Ensure that the space is appropriately prepared.

Welcome Participants

Thank everyone for coming and state it is time to focus on meditation. Ask for cell phones to be completely silenced and set an example by letting others see you doing so. Ask if you are speaking loudly enough for everyone to clearly hear you.

Provide Introductions as Needed

Unless you are certain everyone knows you, tell them your name, your connection with the fraternity, and that you will be facilitating the meditation for this session. Consider whether or not it would be helpful and time-efficient to welcome participants to introduce themselves.

Explain What to Expect

In this session, I am following a script from *The Contemplative Lodge: A Manual for Masons Doing Inner Work Together*, and we will practice a guided imagery meditation on working in a quarry. I will provide structure and detail while leading you through an extended imaginary experience. In effect, you will participate in a story I am telling. Unless I say otherwise, imagine only what I describe, and if other images come up, simply return your attention to imagining what I describe as vividly as possible. This type of meditation intentionally involves complex symbolism with which you can interact to develop your own insights and questions for further contemplation. Are there any questions?

RELAXATION AND CENTERING

Closing your eyes or gazing blankly at some point in front of you, begin to relax and turn your attention inward. If you wish, take a moment to silently invoke the aid of Deity.

Pause for several breaths.

Slowly take in a deep breath, inhaling all the air you can without straining, and then hold it, hold it, hold it. Now release the breath, exhaling all the air you can without straining, and then pause, pause, pause.

Slowly take in a second deep breath, inhaling all the air you can without straining, and then hold it, hold it, hold it. Now release the breath, exhaling all the air you can without straining, and then pause, pause, pause.

Slowly take in a third deep breath, inhaling all the air you can without straining, and then hold it, hold it, hold it. Now release the breath, exhaling all the air you can without straining, and then pause, pause,

pause. Now inhale and let your body breathe in its own peaceful, natural rhythm.

Pause for a couple of breaths.

Attend to the sensation of the earth's gravity pulling down on your body. Feel it pulling your feet against the floor. Feel gravity pulling down in your calves and shins. If you notice any unnecessary tension in those muscles, let it go, and let the pull of gravity take you into a deeper state of calm, peaceful relaxation.

Pause for a couple of breaths.

Feel gravity pulling down in your thighs and buttocks, pulling you into your seat. If you notice any unnecessary tension in those muscles, let it go, and let the pull of gravity take you into a deeper state of calm, peaceful relaxation.

Pause for a couple of breaths.

Feel gravity pulling down in your hips, belly, and lower back. If you notice any unnecessary tension in those muscles, let it go, leaving only what is necessary to keep you sitting in a healthy posture, and let the pull of gravity take you into a deeper state of calm, peaceful relaxation.

Pause for a couple of breaths.

Feel gravity pulling down in your ribcage, chest, and upper back. If you notice any unnecessary tension in those muscles, let it go, leaving only what is necessary to keep you sitting in a healthy posture, and

let the pull of gravity take you into a deeper state of calm, peaceful relaxation.

Pause for a couple of breaths.

Feel gravity pulling down in your shoulders and neck. If you notice any unnecessary tension in those muscles, let it go, leaving only what is necessary to keep you sitting in a healthy posture, and let the pull of gravity take you into a deeper state of calm, peaceful relaxation.

Pause for a couple of breaths.

Feel gravity pulling down in your upper arms, forearms, wrists, and hands. If you notice any unnecessary tension in those muscles, let it go, and let the pull of gravity take you into a deeper state of calm, peaceful relaxation.

Pause for a couple of breaths.

Feel gravity pulling down in your jaw, your tongue, around your mouth, and in your cheeks. Feel gravity pulling down around your eyes and in your brow. Feel gravity pulling down in your scalp on the top of your head, around the sides, and down the back. If you notice any unnecessary tension in those muscles, let it go, leaving only what is necessary to keep you sitting in a healthy posture, and let the pull of gravity take you into a deeper state of calm, peaceful relaxation.

Pause for a couple of breaths.

Now, feel gravity pulling down from the top of your head all the way through every part of your body down to the soles of your feet. If you notice any unnecessary tension anywhere, let it go, leaving only what is necessary to keep you sitting in a healthy posture, and let the pull of gravity take you into a deeper state of calm, peaceful relaxation.

Pause for a couple of breaths.

Turn your attention back to your breath, flowing in and out in its own peaceful, natural rhythm. Simply observe it flowing in and out in its own peaceful, natural rhythm. Feel each breath taking you into a deeper state of calm, peaceful relaxation.

Pause for a few breaths.

You can go into an even deeper state of calm, peaceful relaxation by silently marking the breath with the word "in" as you inhale, and "out" as you exhale: iiiiiinnn, ooouuut. Just continue observing the breath flowing in and out in its own peaceful, natural rhythm as you continue silently repeating: iiiiiinnn, ooouuut. Feel each breath taking you into a deeper state of calm, peaceful relaxation.

Pause for several breaths.

IMAGERY PROCESS

Now imagine yourself surrounded by an arid, rocky landscape on a cool, clear morning, wearing sandals, a tunic, and the rough leather apron of an operative stonemason in ancient times. Around you is a gathering of others dressed much like you. In front of you is a nearly vertical limestone hillside, the diagonal strata of its pale yellow stone separated by thin, green lines of scrubby vegetation. The scent of evergreens wafts with the breeze. At the base of the hillside, the two sides of a heavy, wooden gate are standing open, revealing the dark entrance into a large, underground tunnel. Now take a moment to experience this scene as vividly as possible – the cool, arid landscape, your stonemason's clothing, the others milling around you, and the tunnel entrance in the limestone hillside ahead.

Pause for a few breaths.

The sound of a horn travels out from far down the tunnel, and you hear the sounds of many footsteps and voices. Now you can see figures making their way toward the entrance. As they approach the entrance, you see that they are another group of workers, their clothes and bodies covered in dust. They make their way through your group, and you exchange glances, nods, and greetings with some of those who pass you.

Pause for a few breaths.

As the last of the group leaves the tunnel, your group begins walking toward the entrance, where supervisors are taking note of who is and is not present. You enter the downward-sloping tunnel, and it takes your eyes a while to adjust to the darkness. The footsteps and voices of your group echo through the tunnel. The limestone glows with a deep amber color around simple oil lamps hanging at intervals on the tunnel walls. The air is cool and humid, and you smell damp stone.

Now experience your journey in the tunnel as mindfully and vividly as possible.

Pause for a few breaths.

Farther ahead down the tunnel, you see a slightly brighter glow. Someone is barking orders to pick up the pace. The tunnel leads you into a huge underground cavern lit by the amber glow of many oil lamps. This cavern is King Solomon's Quarry, and you can see a great many stones around the quarry in various sizes and states of preparation, some of them still waiting to be finally cleaved from the cavern walls, and some ready to be dragged up the tunnel and taken to the construction site. The workers in your group begin dispersing through the quarry. To your left, someone calls your name. You turn to see a supervisor motioning for you to approach. As you greet each other, take a good look at this person's face, clothing, and build, and hear their voice. What can you gather about your supervisor's character and attitude?

Pause for a few breaths.

Your supervisor instructs you to follow him and leads you toward the side of the quarry and up to a large, crudely hewn, roughly rectangular stone. It stands a bit taller than you, and its width and depth are a little more than the width of your shoulders. As you examine the stone with your eyes and hands, your supervisor explains it is your project to prepare this rough ashlar for the builders' use. You know the speculative symbolism of this stone, but you do not let that distract from attending to the stone as it is right now. If you wish, feel free to speak with your supervisor about the work while you continue examining the stone's colors, contours, textures, and grain.

Pause for a few breaths.

Now your supervisor points out a set of tools in a wooden box on the quarry floor. He tells you to get to work and strides away to check on the work of others. You look into the box to see what tools are available, recalling the operative and speculative uses of each.

Pause for a few breaths.

From the tools, you select what you need to get started, and then proceed to mindfully work on the rough ashlar, carefully attending to everything you do and its effects on the stone. Now continue to work like this for a while, using different tools as needed.

Pause for at least three minutes.

Your supervisor returns to assess your work, and the two of you discuss your skills, the qualities of the stone, the tools available to you, and how you might make better progress.

Pause for a few breaths.

You grin with the knowledge that the things said between the two of you are about much more than preparing a piece of rock. Your supervisor grins back before again leaving you alone to resume the work.

Pause for a few breaths.

You are so absorbed in your continued work that you lose your sense of time. In occasional breaks, you step back to evaluate your work, moving your eyes and hands over the stone to appraise what you have accomplished, and how much you have remaining to do, and then you get back to work.

Pause for a few breaths.

Suddenly your concentration on the stone is broken by the sound of a horn echoing through the quarry, and you look to your right to see stewards approaching with food and water. You and other workers put down your tools and move to meet them. You all receive your rations, sit, eat, and talk with each other.

Pause for a few breaths.

The break has passed pleasantly, and you have just finished your food and water when the horn blows again. You and the other workers return to your stations. Arriving at your ashlar, you pick up your tools and get back to work.

Pause for a few breaths.

Your supervisor approaches, and you realize you have once again lost track of time because you have been so focused on doing the work. Together you discuss your progress and what you have discovered about the stone's qualities while working on it.

Pause for a few breaths.

The horn blows again, and your supervisor shakes your hand and pats you on the back, congratulating you for doing good work. You thank your supervisor and begin moving toward the bottom end of the tunnel with the other workers. You hear your group's voices and footsteps reverberating in the tunnel as you ascend its slope. Up ahead you see the blue sky through the tunnel's entrance, and you can just make out the next group of workers waiting for you to pass. You squint as your eyes adjust to the light and pass through the wooden gates into the early evening air. You notice that the air is warmer, drier, and fragrant with the scent of fresh air and evergreens. Passing through the waiting group, you exchange greetings with some of them and pause to turn and watch them begin the trek down into the tunnel. As you stand there, you recall your work on the rough ashlar. You are aware of how you feel about what you have done, and you begin to reflect more on its speculative symbolism.

Pause for a few breaths.

RECONNECT WITH THE PRESENT AND END THE MEDITATION

Release the imagery and again clear your mind as you attend to the sensations of your body right here. Feel gravity pulling you down into your seat and your feet against the floor. Feel the air on your skin and your breath flowing in and out. Hear what you hear. Smell what you smell and taste what you taste. When you are ready, open your eyes and see what you see.

The meditation has ended. Feel free to move and stretch your limbs.

REFLECTION

Invite participants to share their experiences, insights, and questions. Remember to use these skills:

- *welcoming sharing*

- *active listening*

- *scanning the group*

- *managing the flow*

- *being careful with advice*

WRAP UP AND CLOSE

Announce that it is time to end the session. Restate some of the more common or poignant reflections. Inform participants about the next time and location for meditation or other contemplative activities. Thank everyone for their participation.

GUIDED IMAGERY SCRIPT #3: TRAVELING TO PRUDENTIA

Become thoroughly familiar with this script before using it to facilitate an activity. Notes and additional guidelines for the facilitator appear in italics, and spoken parts are indicated by a regular font. Consider your audience and what, if any, adjustments you might make in facilitating this activity. Ensure that the space is appropriately prepared. It can be very helpful to provide participants a traditional image of Prudence in the form of a woman with a mirror and serpent.

WELCOME PARTICIPANTS

Thank everyone for coming and state it is time to focus on meditation. Ask for cell phones to be completely silenced and set an example by letting others see you doing so. Ask if you are speaking loudly enough for everyone to clearly hear you.

PROVIDE INTRODUCTIONS AS NEEDED

Unless you are certain everyone knows you, tell them your name, your connection with the fraternity, and that you will be facilitating the meditation for this session. Consider whether or not it would be helpful and time-efficient to welcome participants to introduce themselves.

EXPLAIN WHAT TO EXPECT

In this session, I am following a script from *The Contemplative Lodge: A Manual for Masons Doing Inner Work Together*, and we will practice a guided imagery meditation on the Cardinal Virtue of Prudence. We will interact with Prudence in a human form as often presented in Masonry as well as in much older traditions. I will provide structure and detail while leading you through an extended imaginary experience. In effect, you will participate in a story I am telling. Unless I say otherwise, imagine only what I describe, and if other images come up, simply return your attention to imagining what I describe as vividly as possible. This type of meditation intentionally involves complex symbolism with which you can interact to develop your own insights and questions for further contemplation. Are there any questions?

RELAXATION AND CENTERING

Closing your eyes or gazing blankly at some point in front of you, begin to relax and turn your attention inward. If you wish, take a moment to silently invoke the aid of Deity.

Pause for several breaths.

Slowly take in a deep breath, inhaling all the air you can without straining, and then hold it, hold it, hold it. Now release the breath, exhaling all the air you can without straining, and then pause, pause, pause.

Slowly take in a second deep breath, inhaling all the air you can without straining, and then hold it, hold it, hold it. Now release the breath, exhaling all the air you can without straining, and then pause, pause, pause.

Slowly take in a third deep breath, inhaling all the air you can without straining, and then hold it, hold it, hold it. Now release the breath, exhaling all the air you can without straining, and then pause, pause, pause. Now inhale and let your body breathe in its own peaceful, natural rhythm.

Pause for a couple of breaths.

Attend to the sensation of the earth's gravity pulling down on your body. Feel it pulling your feet against the floor. Feel gravity pulling down in your calves and shins. If you notice any unnecessary tension in those muscles, let it go, and let the pull of gravity take you into a deeper state of calm, peaceful relaxation.

Pause for a couple of breaths.

Feel gravity pulling down in your thighs and buttocks, pulling you into your seat. If you notice any unnecessary tension in those muscles, let it go, and let the pull of gravity take you into a deeper state of calm, peaceful relaxation.

Pause for a couple of breaths.

Feel gravity pulling down in your hips, belly, and lower back. If you notice any unnecessary tension in those muscles, let it go, leaving only what is necessary to keep you sitting in a healthy posture, and let the pull of gravity take you into a deeper state of calm, peaceful relaxation.

Pause for a couple of breaths.

Feel gravity pulling down in your ribcage, chest, and upper back. If you notice any unnecessary tension in those muscles, let it go, leaving only what is necessary to keep you sitting in a healthy posture, and let the pull of gravity take you into a deeper state of calm, peaceful relaxation.

Pause for a couple of breaths.

Feel gravity pulling down in your shoulders and neck. If you notice any unnecessary tension in those muscles, let it go, leaving only what is necessary to keep you sitting in a healthy posture, and let the pull of gravity take you into a deeper state of calm, peaceful relaxation.

Pause for a couple of breaths.

Feel gravity pulling down in your upper arms, forearms, wrists, and hands. If you notice any unnecessary tension in those muscles, let it go, and let the pull of gravity take you into a deeper state of calm, peaceful relaxation.

Pause for a couple of breaths.

Feel gravity pulling down in your jaw, your tongue, around your mouth, and in your cheeks. Feel gravity pulling down around your eyes and in your brow. Feel gravity pulling down in your scalp on the top of your head, around the sides, and down the back. If you notice any unnecessary tension in those muscles, let it go, leaving only what

is necessary to keep you sitting in a healthy posture, and let the pull of gravity take you into a deeper state of calm, peaceful relaxation.

Pause for a couple of breaths.

Now, feel gravity pulling down from the top of your head all the way through every part of your body down to the soles of your feet. If you notice any unnecessary tension anywhere, let it go, leaving only what is necessary to keep you sitting in a healthy posture, and let the pull of gravity take you into a deeper state of calm, peaceful relaxation.

Pause for a couple of breaths.

Turn your attention back to your breath, flowing in and out in its own peaceful, natural rhythm. Simply observe it flowing in and out in its own peaceful, natural rhythm. Feel each breath taking you into a deeper state of calm, peaceful relaxation.

Pause for a few breaths.

You can go into an even deeper state of calm, peaceful relaxation by silently marking the breath with the word "in" as you inhale, and "out" as you exhale: iiiiiinnn, ooouuut. Just continue observing the breath flowing in and out in its own peaceful, natural rhythm as you continue silently repeating: iiiiiinnn, ooouuut. Feel each breath taking you into a deeper state of calm, peaceful relaxation.

Pause for several breaths.

IMAGERY PROCESS

Now imagine yourself in the pre-dawn darkness facing east toward the edge of a dense forest, carrying a lantern. An owl's hoot echoes through the woods. Your lantern's light reveals that you are on a narrow, barely discernable path marked with a sign that reads "Prudentia" and is marked with an arrow pointing ahead. Above you is a clear, indigo sky dotted with the lights of stars and planets. Behind you, in the west, a waxing and nearly full moon is descending toward the black horizon. You again face the woods and begin following the path. It winds like a serpent through the trees and is so faint that you must keep your eyes on it and your lantern held low, and you continue traveling through the woods.

Pause for a few breaths.

The ground becomes rockier, and the path even harder to discern. Just as you begin to fear you will lose your way, you discover the path has led you to the mouth of a cave. Here there is another sign for Prudentia, and it indicates that you must continue into the cave. You stretch your lantern out before you and walk into the cave. It is cool and cobwebbed, and there are many passageways leading off into different directions. At times you may question whether you are still on the path to Prudentia, but you continue making your way ahead.

Pause for a couple of breaths.

As you proceed, the stone ceiling above you slopes lower and lower, and you must stoop down. Eventually, you are stooping so low that you are forced onto your hands and knees, moving the lantern ahead of you as you go. The air grows thick and musty, and with it grow your doubts about your direction. But you are determined to persevere, continuing to crawl toward your goal.

Pause for a couple of breaths.

Suddenly the path slopes sharply downward, and you tumble head over heels into a chamber. Fortunately, your lantern remains unbroken, and, as you regain your bearing, you see before you the skull, clothing, and bones of some poor traveler whose journey ended here. As you contemplate those lifeless eyes and that soulless grin, a glimmer in your peripheral vision grabs your attention. You get back on your feet and hold up the lantern to see colorful veins of crystals and precious metals reflecting the light from the chamber walls. You take a moment to wonder at the otherworldly beauty and ponder the potential wealth it offers.

Pause for a couple of breaths.

As you examine the chamber walls, you notice gashes and gouges that could only have been made by tools. Once again, the skeleton comes within your lantern's light, and you nod with understanding as you now see its midsection was crushed under a large rock, with mining tools lying beside the remains. For a moment you kneel to wish peace to the soul of the miner and reflect on some of the lessons to be learned from this scene.

Pause for a few breaths.

Pressing on, you find the only way out of the chamber, other than the way you entered, and crawl through it to discover a passageway sloping upward that grows large enough for you to once again walk on without stooping. In the darkness ahead you hear a sound and recognize it as the rushing of water. It grows louder and louder as you continue to move forward. Following the passageway as it turns to the right, you enter a high, domed cavern where your lantern's light is reflected by a large pool of water at the base of a great subterranean waterfall. For a moment you stand there, allowing yourself to feel awe at the sight.

Pause for a couple of breaths.

Considering the continuation of your journey, you look around and see that the steep smooth walls of the cavern completely encircle the pool, and there is no way forward except into the pool and toward the falls, where the rock wall is rougher and possibly climbable. Determined to press on, you wade into the cold water, uncertain of its depth or what might be beneath the surface. The floor of the pool slopes downward and is slippery. Soon you are in up to your chest, holding the lantern at shoulder level. You are not yet halfway to the falls.

Pause for a couple of breaths.

You pass the halfway point in the pool. You are in up to your chin, shivering and struggling to hold the lantern above your head, hoping the pool grows no deeper and wondering if your goal of going to Prudentia is worth this risk. Suddenly something brushes across the front of your hips, startling you and giving you the energy to move faster.

Pause for a breath.

As you get close to the falls, a cold spray stings your face, and waves lap at your nose. The lantern feels heavier and heavier. To the left of the falls you can see a ledge at the waterline. Reaching it, you are relieved to find it is large enough for you to set the lantern down and crawl up out of the water, to sit and gather your wits.

Pause for a couple of breaths.

Looking at the falls from the side, you are excited to see that behind its veil is another passageway, and you hope it offers a way forward rather than attempting the long dangerous climb up and into the stream pouring from the black hole above. Rising to your feet and picking up your lantern, you slip behind the veil and begin moving on, reflecting on the perils through which you have just passed.

Pause for a few of breaths.

As you continue walking, the passageway slopes more steeply upward and you enjoy the warm breeze that dries your clothes and warms your bones. In the darkness ahead, you see a very dim glow of purple light, and within a few more steps you realize that it is the twilight sky visible through an opening ahead.

Pause for a couple of breaths.

You step out onto a cliff overlooking a deeply shadowed valley, and in the distance ahead, the Morning Star gleams brightly above the eastern horizon, which is beginning to glow with the colors of the coming dawn. It is a lovely sight to behold.

Pause for a couple of breaths.

Looking around, you find that the cliff on which you are standing is just beneath the tree line of a rugged, windswept peak. Near the top is a small building. To your right is another Prudentia trail sign, and its arrow points up toward that building. You start on the path, its switchbacks zigzagging up the steep, rocky slope. The air grows thinner, and the winds blow stronger across the face of the mountain. At times, you must take your steps very carefully to avoid becoming exhausted, being blown over, and tumbling down. You persevere and keep hiking up the mountain.

Pause for a couple of breaths.

As you approach the building, you see that it is a rectangular structure, about twice as long as it is tall and wide. It is situated east to west and constructed of squared and finished stones. A stone column stands on either side of the simple wooden door on its eastern end. The winds quickly subside as you hike higher toward the building. Approaching the stone columns, the air becomes still and peaceful, and you see a sign above the door that reads "Prudentia." You knock on the door, but there is no answer. You open the door, holding your lantern in front of you, and step in, leaving the door open behind you. At the center of the room is a perfectly squared and polished cubical stone, standing about knee high. It is a perfect ashlar serving as an altar. Above the cubical stone a short chain hangs from the ceiling. You realize its pupose is for hanging a lantern, and so you step forward, lift your lantern up, and leave it on the chain's hook. Now you see a circle of eight words engraved into the top of the cube. The eight words are acumen, caution, circumspection, foresight, intelligence, memory, reason, and receptivity. The lantern light also reveals that the western wall across from you bears this statement: "Wisdom seeks the secret shade, the lonely cell designed for contemplation. There enthroned she sits, delivering her sacred oracles. There let us seek her and pursue the real bliss. Though the passage be difficult, the farther we trace it, the easier it will become."

Beneath the statement is a simple, wooden chair, and you move to sit and rest there. Sitting and facing east, looking over the cubical stone and through the open door, you see the predawn horizon has become much brighter, with beautiful rays reaching up like fingers from the still hidden sun. Above the door is a metal plate inscribed with the words "Know Thyself." Your eyes return to the majestic horizon, and you become still to mindfully watch for the break of dawn.

Pause for a couple of breaths.

Now the first bright golden spark of the sun peeks over the horizon. Its beam of light reaches in through the door to illuminate the cubical stone, mingling with the glow of your lantern. In this weaving of light, something miraculous begins to happen. Colorful rays begin to swirl around each other, spiraling up and down between the lantern and altar, gradually giving form to a dignified woman, sitting upon the cubical stone and facing you. In her left hand she holds a serpent. In her right hand is a mirror. You watch for a moment as she fully materializes.

Pause for a couple of breaths.

At last Prudentia sits before you as a living, breathing woman, and you rise from your chair to respectfully greet her. She smiles, nods, and invites you to approach and raise any matter you wish. You may now take some time to communicate with her, noticing how she occasionally glances into her mirror before responding to you.

Pause for a few minutes.

Now the two of you come to a pause, sensing it is nearly time to end this communication. Silently looking into your eyes, Prudentia motions for you to come closer to her, and you know she has one last thing of importance to share with you. She turns her mirror toward you, inviting you to look. The image of your face quickly dissipates, and something else takes its place. Whatever you see, it is something Prudentia knows you need to see and contemplate.

Pause for several breaths.

She turns her mirror back toward herself and elegantly nods to bid you farewell. As you express your gratitude and farewell to her, Prudentia's form begins transitioning back into swirling bands of light, gradually dissolving and dissipating, leaving you with a splendid view of the top half of the sun's golden disk now risen over the horizon.

You smile and close your eyes to enjoy its warmth radiating into your face, neck, and chest.

Pause for a couple of breaths.

RECONNECT WITH THE PRESENT AND END THE MEDITATION

Release the imagery and again clear your mind as you attend to the sensations of your body right here. Feel gravity pulling you down into your seat and your feet against the floor. Feel the air on your skin and your breath flowing in and out. Hear what you hear. Smell what you smell and taste what you taste. When you are ready, open your eyes and see what you see.

The meditation has ended. Feel free to move and stretch your limbs.

REFLECTION

Invite participants to share their experiences, insights, and questions. Remember to use these skills:

- *welcoming sharing*
- *active listening*
- *scanning the group*
- *managing the flow*
- *being careful with advice*

WRAP UP AND CLOSE

Announce that it is time to end the session. Restate some of the more common or poignant reflections. Inform participants about the next time and location for meditation or other contemplative activities. Thank everyone for their participation.

ENERGY WORK SCRIPT #1: PRECIOUS OINTMENT

Become thoroughly familiar with this script before using it to facilitate an activity. Notes and additional guidelines for the facilitator appear in italics, and spoken parts are indicated by a regular font. Consider your audience and what, if any, adjustments you might make in facilitating this activity. Ensure that the space is appropriately prepared.

WELCOME PARTICIPANTS

Thank everyone for coming and state it is time to focus on meditation. Ask for cell phones to be completely silenced and set an example by letting others see you doing so. Ask if you are speaking loudly enough for everyone to clearly hear you.

PROVIDE INTRODUCTIONS AS NEEDED

Unless you are certain everyone knows you, tell them your name, your connection with the fraternity, and that you will be facilitating the meditation for this session. Consider whether or not it would be helpful and time-efficient to welcome participants to introduce themselves.

EXPLAIN WHAT TO EXPECT

In this session, I am following a script from *The Contemplative Lodge: A Manual for Masons Doing Inner Work Together*. We will use breath and imagery to enhance our experience of Psalm 133, focusing on energy centers at the heart and crown of the head. Unless I say otherwise, imagine only what I describe, and if other images come up, simply return your attention to imagining what I describe as vividly as possible. Are there any questions?

RELAXATION AND CENTERING

Closing your eyes or gazing blankly at some point in front of you, begin to relax and turn your attention inward. If you wish, take a moment to silently invoke the aid of Deity.

Pause for several breaths.

Slowly take in a deep breath, inhaling all the air you can without straining, and then hold it, hold it, hold it. Now release the breath, exhaling all the air you can without straining, and then pause, pause, pause.

Slowly take in a second deep breath, inhaling all the air you can without straining, and then hold it, hold it, hold it. Now release the breath, exhaling all the air you can without straining, and then pause, pause, pause.

Slowly take in a third deep breath, inhaling all the air you can without straining, and then hold it, hold it, hold it. Now release the breath, exhaling all the air you can without straining, and then pause, pause, pause. Now inhale and let your body breathe in its own peaceful, natural rhythm.

Pause for a couple of breaths.

Attend to the sensation of the earth's gravity pulling down on your body. Feel it pulling your feet against the floor. Feel gravity pulling down in your calves and shins. If you notice any unnecessary tension in those muscles, let it go, and let the pull of gravity take you into a deeper state of calm, peaceful relaxation.

Pause for a couple of breaths.

Feel gravity pulling down in your thighs and buttocks, pulling you into your seat. If you notice any unnecessary tension in those muscles, let it go, and let the pull of gravity take you into a deeper state of calm, peaceful relaxation.

Pause for a couple of breaths.

Feel gravity pulling down in your hips, belly, and lower back. If you notice any unnecessary tension in those muscles, let it go, leaving only what is necessary to keep you sitting in a healthy posture, and let the pull of gravity take you into a deeper state of calm, peaceful relaxation.

Pause for a couple of breaths.

Feel gravity pulling down in your ribcage, chest, and upper back. If you notice any unnecessary tension in those muscles, let it go, leaving only what is necessary to keep you sitting in a healthy posture, and let the pull of gravity take you into a deeper state of calm, peaceful relaxation.

Pause for a couple of breaths.

Feel gravity pulling down in your shoulders and neck. If you notice any unnecessary tension in those muscles, let it go, leaving only what

is necessary to keep you sitting in a healthy posture, and let the pull of gravity take you into a deeper state of calm, peaceful relaxation.

Pause for a couple of breaths.

Feel gravity pulling down in your upper arms, forearms, wrists, and hands. If you notice any unnecessary tension in those muscles, let it go, and let the pull of gravity take you into a deeper state of calm, peaceful relaxation.

Pause for a couple of breaths.

Feel gravity pulling down in your jaw, your tongue, around your mouth, and in your cheeks. Feel gravity pulling down around your eyes and in your brow. Feel gravity pulling down in your scalp on the top of your head, around the sides, and down the back. If you notice any unnecessary tension in those muscles, let it go, leaving only what is necessary to keep you sitting in a healthy posture, and let the pull of gravity take you into a deeper state of calm, peaceful relaxation.

Pause for a couple of breaths.

Now, feel gravity pulling down from the top of your head all the way through every part of your body down to the soles of your feet. If you notice any unnecessary tension anywhere, let it go, leaving only what is necessary to keep you sitting in a healthy posture, and let the pull of gravity take you into a deeper state of calm, peaceful relaxation.

Pause for a couple of breaths.

Turn your attention back to your breath, flowing in and out in its own peaceful, natural rhythm. Simply observe it flowing in and out in its own peaceful, natural rhythm. Feel each breath taking you into a deeper state of calm, peaceful relaxation.

Pause for a few breaths.

You can go into an even deeper state of calm, peaceful relaxation by silently marking the breath with the word "in" as you inhale, and "out" as you exhale: iiiiiinnn, ooouuut. Just continue observing the breath flowing in and out in its own peaceful, natural rhythm as you continue silently repeating: iiiiiinnn, ooouuut. Feel each breath taking you into a deeper state of calm, peaceful relaxation.

Pause for several breaths.

ENERGY WORK PROCESS

Focus your attention on your heart and allow the appropriate feelings to grow there as you meditate upon these words:

Behold, how good and how pleasant it is for brethren to dwell together in unity.

Pause for a couple of breaths.

Feel that good and pleasant sense of togetherness in your heart and imagine it as a ball of glowing, white light in and around your heart.

Pause for a few breaths.

Now take a deep breath as you imagine another ball appearing at the top of your head.

Pause for a couple of breaths.

Try to feel its energy radiating onto your scalp in some way, such as warmth or electricity.

Pause for a couple of breaths.

Now try to actually feel on your own body what these words describe:

It is like the precious ointment upon the head that ran down upon the beard, even Aaron's beard, that went down to the skirts of his garments.

Pause for a couple of breaths.

As the dew of Hermon, and as the dew that descended upon the mountains of Zion, for there the Lord commanded the blessing, even life forevermore.

Pause for a few breaths.

One again, focus your attention on the ball of energy in and around your heart and allow the appropriate feelings to grow there as you meditate upon these words:

Behold, how good and how pleasant it is for brethren to dwell together in unity.

Pause for a couple of breaths.

Feel that good and pleasant sense of togetherness in your heart and imagine it radiating from the ball of glowing, white light in and around your heart.

Pause for a couple of breaths.

Now take a deep breath as you move your attention to the ball of energy at the top of your head.

Pause for a couple of breaths.

Try to feel its energy radiating onto your scalp.

Pause for a couple of breaths.

Now try to actually feel on your own body what these words describe:

It is like the precious ointment upon the head that ran down upon the beard, even Aaron's beard, that went down to the skirts of his garments.

Pause for a couple of breaths.

As the dew of Hermon, and as the dew that descended upon the mountains of Zion, for there the Lord commanded the blessing, even life forevermore.

Pause for a few breaths.

A third time, focus your attention on the ball of energy in and around your heart and allow the appropriate feelings to grow there as you meditate upon these words:

Behold, how good and how pleasant it is for brethren to dwell together in unity.

Pause for a couple of breaths.

Feel that good and pleasant sense of togetherness in your heart and imagine it radiating out from the ball of glowing white light in and around your heart.

Pause for a couple of breaths.

Now take a deep breath as you return your attention to the ball of energy at the top of your head.

Pause for a couple of breaths.

Try to feel its energy radiating onto your scalp.

Pause for a couple of breaths.

Now try to actually feel on your own body what these words describe:

It is like the precious ointment upon the head that ran down upon the beard, even Aaron's beard, that went down to the skirts of his garments.

Pause for a couple of breaths.

As the dew of Hermon, and as the dew that descended upon the mountains of Zion, for there the Lord commanded the blessing, even life forevermore.

Pause for a few breaths.

Now I will simply recite the words, and you may follow along with the imagery and breathwork without prompting.

Behold, how good and how pleasant it is for brethren to dwell together in unity.

Pause for a couple of breaths.

It is like the precious ointment upon the head that ran down upon the beard, even Aaron's beard, that went down to the skirts of his garments, as the dew of Hermon, and as the dew that descended upon the mountains of Zion, for there the Lord commanded the blessing, even life forevermore.

Pause for a few breaths.

Behold, how good and how pleasant it is for brethren to dwell together in unity.

Pause for a couple of breaths.

It is like the precious ointment upon the head that ran down upon the beard, even Aaron's beard, that went down to the skirts of his garments, as the dew of Hermon, and as the dew that descended upon the mountains of Zion, for there the Lord commanded the blessing, even life forevermore.

Pause for a few breaths.

Now we will have some time in silence in which you may continue the energy process on your own or sit in reflection on what you have experienced.

Pause for several minutes.

RECONNECT WITH THE PRESENT AND END THE MEDITATION

Release the imagery and again clear your mind as you attend to the sensations of your body right here. Feel gravity pulling you down into your seat and your feet against the floor. Feel the air on your skin and your breath flowing in and out. Hear what you hear. Smell what you smell and taste what you taste. When you are ready, open your eyes and see what you see.

The meditation has ended. Feel free to move and stretch your limbs.

REFLECTION

Invite participants to share their experiences, insights, and questions. Remember to use these skills:

- *welcoming sharing*

- *active listening*

- *scanning the group*

- *managing the flow*

- *being careful with advice*

WRAP UP AND CLOSE

Announce that it is time to end the session. Restate some of the more common or poignant reflections. Inform participants about the next time and location for meditation or other contemplative activities. Thank everyone for their participation.

ENERGY WORK SCRIPT #2: ENERGIZING THE PLUMB LINE

Become thoroughly familiar with this script before using it to facilitate an activity. Notes and additional guidelines for the facilitator appear in italics, and spoken parts are indicated by a regular font. Consider your audience and what, if any, adjustments you might make in facilitating this activity. Ensure that the space is appropriately prepared.

WELCOME PARTICIPANTS

Thank everyone for coming and state it is time to focus on meditation. Ask for cell phones to be completely silenced and set an example by letting others see you doing so. Ask if you are speaking loudly enough for everyone to clearly hear you.

PROVIDE INTRODUCTIONS AS NEEDED

Unless you are certain everyone knows you, tell them your name, your connection with the fraternity, and that you will be facilitating the meditation for this session. Consider whether or not it would be helpful and time-efficient to welcome participants to introduce themselves.

EXPLAIN WHAT TO EXPECT

In this session, I am following a script from *The Contemplative Lodge: A Manual for Masons Doing Inner Work Together*, and we will use breath and light in a basic way of working with subtle energy. I will provide structure and detail to allow you to experience the presence, amplification, and circulation of energy within you. When we do the circulation, you will imagine energy moving in and around you in a spiraling motion from left to front to right to rear, first down from the top and then up from the bottom.

Illustrate the spiraling movement with your hands.

Unless I say otherwise, imagine only what I describe, and if other images come up, simply return your attention to imagining what I describe as vividly as possible. Are there any questions?

RELAXATION AND CENTERING

Closing your eyes or gazing blankly at some point in front of you, begin to relax and turn your attention inward. If you wish, take a moment to silently invoke the aid of Deity.

Pause for several breaths.

Slowly take in a deep breath, inhaling all the air you can without straining, and then hold it, hold it, hold it. Now release the breath, exhaling all the air you can without straining, and then pause, pause, pause.

Slowly take in a second deep breath, inhaling all the air you can without straining, and then hold it, hold it, hold it. Now release the breath, exhaling all the air you can without straining, and then pause, pause, pause.

Slowly take in a third deep breath, inhaling all the air you can without straining, and then hold it, hold it, hold it. Now release the breath, exhaling all the air you can without straining, and then pause, pause, pause. Now inhale and let your body breathe in its own peaceful, natural rhythm.

Pause for a couple of breaths.

Attend to the sensation of the earth's gravity pulling down on your body. Feel it pulling your feet against the floor. Feel gravity pulling down in your calves and shins. If you notice any unnecessary tension in those muscles, let it go, and let the pull of gravity take you into a deeper state of calm, peaceful relaxation.

Pause for a couple of breaths.

Feel gravity pulling down in your thighs and buttocks, pulling you into your seat. If you notice any unnecessary tension in those muscles, let it go, and let the pull of gravity take you into a deeper state of calm, peaceful relaxation.

Pause for a couple of breaths.

Feel gravity pulling down in your hips, belly, and lower back. If you notice any unnecessary tension in those muscles, let it go, leaving only what is necessary to keep you sitting in a healthy posture, and let the pull of gravity take you into a deeper state of calm, peaceful relaxation.

Pause for a couple of breaths.

Feel gravity pulling down in your ribcage, chest, and upper back. If you notice any unnecessary tension in those muscles, let it go, leaving only what is necessary to keep you sitting in a healthy posture, and let the pull of gravity take you into a deeper state of calm, peaceful relaxation.

Pause for a couple of breaths.

Feel gravity pulling down in your shoulders and neck. If you notice any unnecessary tension in those muscles, let it go, leaving only what is necessary to keep you sitting in a healthy posture, and let the pull of gravity take you into a deeper state of calm, peaceful relaxation.

Pause for a couple of breaths.

Feel gravity pulling down in your upper arms, forearms, wrists, and hands. If you notice any unnecessary tension in those muscles, let it go, and let the pull of gravity take you into a deeper state of calm, peaceful relaxation.

Pause for a couple of breaths.

Feel gravity pulling down in your jaw, your tongue, around your mouth, and in your cheeks. Feel gravity pulling down around your eyes and in your brow. Feel gravity pulling down in your scalp on the top of your head, around the sides, and down the back. If you notice any unnecessary tension in those muscles, let it go, leaving only what is necessary to keep you sitting in a healthy posture, and let the pull of gravity take you into a deeper state of calm, peaceful relaxation.

Pause for a couple of breaths.

Now, feel gravity pulling down from the top of your head all the way through every part of your body down to the soles of your feet. If you notice any unnecessary tension anywhere, let it go, leaving only what is necessary to keep you sitting in a healthy posture, and let the pull of gravity take you into a deeper state of calm, peaceful relaxation.

Pause for a couple of breaths.

Turn your attention back to your breath, flowing in and out in its own peaceful, natural rhythm. Simply observe it flowing in and out in its own peaceful, natural rhythm. Feel each breath taking you into a deeper state of calm, peaceful relaxation.

Pause for a few breaths.

You can go into an even deeper state of calm, peaceful relaxation by silently marking the breath with the word "in" as you inhale, and "out" as you exhale: iiiiiinnn, ooouuut. Just continue observing the breath flowing in and out in its own peaceful, natural rhythm as you continue silently repeating: iiiiiinnn, ooouuut. Feel each breath taking you into a deeper state of calm, peaceful relaxation.

Pause for several breaths.

ENERGY WORK PROCESS

Imagine a plumb line, a small straight line, of brilliant white light running into the top of your head from the highest heavens, and down through your body into the depths of the Earth. Try to experience the presence of this plumb line as something like a magnetic or electrical current flowing between the highest heavens and the center of the Earth.

Pause for a few breaths.

As you focus on the plumb line, with each breath make it gradually grow in diameter so that, after several breaths, it has become a column of light with a circumference as large as your own head, penetrating down through your body and organs. Feel the pure white light as warm, cleansing, healing, and energizing.

Pause for several breaths.

Now inhale deeply and, as you exhale, imagine that with your breath even more energy is spiraling around the plumb line down from the top of your head, through your body into the earth below. The spiraling motion is from left to front to right to rear. As you inhale, imagine that the energy is spiraling up around the plumb line from the bottom of your seat, through your body and into the heavens above. The spiraling motion is again from left to front to right to rear. As you exhale deeply, the energy spirals down around the plumb line, from left to front to right to rear. As you inhale, it spirals up around the plumb line, from left to front to right to rear. Inhaling, it spirals up. Exhaling, it spirals down. Continue repeating this process on your own.

Pause for about a dozen breaths.

Now, stop circulating the energy and breathe naturally, continuing to imagine the brilliant white plumb line running through your body between the highest heavens and the center of the Earth. Attend to any effects this work has on your body, emotions, and thoughts.

RECONNECT WITH THE PRESENT AND END THE MEDITATION

Release the imagery and again clear your mind as you attend to the sensations of your body right here. Feel gravity pulling you down into your seat and your feet against the floor. Feel the air on your skin and your breath flowing in and out. Hear what you hear. Smell what you smell and taste what you taste. When you are ready, open your eyes and see what you see.

The meditation has ended. Feel free to move and stretch your limbs.

REFLECTION

Invite participants to share their experiences, insights, and questions. Remember to use these skills:

- *welcoming sharing*
- *active listening*
- *scanning the group*
- *managing the flow*
- *being careful with advice*

WRAP UP AND CLOSE

Announce that it is time to end the session. Restate some of the more common or poignant reflections. Inform participants about the next time and location for meditation or other contemplative activities. Thank everyone for their participation.

Energy Work Script #3: Integrating the Elements

Become thoroughly familiar with this script before using it to facilitate an activity. Notes and additional guidelines for the facilitator appear in italics, and spoken parts are indicated by a regular font. Consider your audience and what, if any, adjustments you might make in facilitating this activity. Ensure that the space is appropriately prepared.

Welcome Participants

Thank everyone for coming and state it is time to focus on meditation. Ask for cell phones to be completely silenced and set an example by letting others see you doing so. Ask if you are speaking loudly enough for everyone to clearly hear you.

Provide Introductions as Needed

Unless you are certain everyone knows you, tell them your name, your connection with the fraternity, and that you will be facilitating the meditation for this session. Consider whether or not it would be helpful and time-efficient to welcome participants to introduce themselves.

Explain What to Expect

In this session, I am following a script from *The Contemplative Lodge: A Manual for Masons Doing Inner Work Together*. We will use breath, imagery, and sound to explore and integrate the energies of the four classical elements – earth, water, fire, and air – as well as aether or spirit. The chanting will be done with five vowel sounds: UH, as in mud, for earth; OO, as in cool, for water; OH, as in go, for fire; AH, as in calm, for air; and I, as in tie, for aether. Unless I say otherwise, imagine only what I describe, and if other images come up, then simply return your attention to imagining what I describe as vividly as possible. Are there any questions?

RELAXATION AND CENTERING

Closing your eyes or gazing blankly at some point in front of you, begin to relax and turn your attention inward. If you wish, take a moment to silently invoke the aid of Deity.

Pause for several breaths.

Slowly take in a deep breath, inhaling all the air you can without straining, and then hold it, hold it, hold it. Now release the breath, exhaling all the air you can without straining, and then pause, pause, pause.

Slowly take in a second deep breath, inhaling all the air you can without straining, and then hold it, hold it, hold it. Now release the breath, exhaling all the air you can without straining, and then pause, pause, pause.

Slowly take in a third deep breath, inhaling all the air you can without straining, and then hold it, hold it, hold it. Now release the breath, exhaling all the air you can without straining, and then pause, pause,

pause. Now inhale and let your body breathe in its own peaceful, natural rhythm.

Pause for a couple of breaths.

Attend to the sensation of the earth's gravity pulling down on your body. Feel it pulling your feet against the floor. Feel gravity pulling down in your calves and shins. If you notice any unnecessary tension in those muscles, let it go, and let the pull of gravity take you into a deeper state of calm, peaceful relaxation.

Pause for a couple of breaths.

Feel gravity pulling down in your thighs and buttocks, pulling you into your seat. If you notice any unnecessary tension in those muscles, let it go, and let the pull of gravity take you into a deeper state of calm, peaceful relaxation.

Pause for a couple of breaths.

Feel gravity pulling down in your hips, belly, and lower back. If you notice any unnecessary tension in those muscles, let it go, leaving only what is necessary to keep you sitting in a healthy posture, and let the pull of gravity take you into a deeper state of calm, peaceful relaxation.

Pause for a couple of breaths.

Feel gravity pulling down in your ribcage, chest, and upper back. If you notice any unnecessary tension in those muscles, let it go, leaving only what is necessary to keep you sitting in a healthy posture, and let the pull of gravity take you into a deeper state of calm, peaceful relaxation.

Pause for a couple of breaths.

Feel gravity pulling down in your shoulders and neck. If you notice any unnecessary tension in those muscles, let it go, leaving only what is necessary to keep you sitting in a healthy posture, and let the pull of gravity take you into a deeper state of calm, peaceful relaxation.

Pause for a couple of breaths.

Feel gravity pulling down in your upper arms, forearms, wrists, and hands. If you notice any unnecessary tension in those muscles, let it go, and let the pull of gravity take you into a deeper state of calm, peaceful relaxation.

Pause for a couple of breaths.

Feel gravity pulling down in your jaw, your tongue, around your mouth, and in your cheeks. Feel gravity pulling down around your eyes and in your brow. Feel gravity pulling down in your scalp on the top of your head, around the sides, and down the back. If you notice any unnecessary tension in those muscles, let it go, leaving only what

is necessary to keep you sitting in a healthy posture, and let the pull of gravity take you into a deeper state of calm, peaceful relaxation.

Pause for a couple of breaths.

Now, feel gravity pulling down from the top of your head all the way through every part of your body down to the soles of your feet. If you notice any unnecessary tension anywhere, let it go, leaving only what is necessary to keep you sitting in a healthy posture, and let the pull of gravity take you into a deeper state of calm, peaceful relaxation.

Pause for a couple of breaths.

Turn your attention back to your breath, flowing in and out in its own peaceful, natural rhythm. Simply observe it flowing in and out in its own peaceful, natural rhythm. Feel each breath taking you into a deeper state of calm, peaceful relaxation.

Pause for a few breaths.

You can go into an even deeper state of calm, peaceful relaxation by silently marking the breath with the word "in" as you inhale, and "out" as you exhale: iiiiiinnn, ooouuut. Just continue observing the breath flowing in and out in its own peaceful, natural rhythm as you continue silently repeating: iiiiiinnn, ooouuut. Feel each breath taking you into a deeper state of calm, peaceful relaxation.

Pause for several breaths.

ENERGY WORK PROCESS

Now focus on the tip of your tailbone, a place corresponding to the element of earth. In a moment, we will begin chanting the vowel sound UH and, as we do so, imagine yourself becoming even more a creature of earth, getting colder and colder, your flesh and bones getting drier and harder, making you feel heavier and heavier, less and less mobile. Yet these changes are comfortable and welcome, as you desire to more fully experience the special energies of earth. We are about to begin the chant.

Begin the chant uuuuhhhh and continue through at least five repetitions.

Rest and continue the chant silently within, while seeing and feeling your body crystallizing into one of stone – solid, heavy, cold, and dry.

Pause for a few breaths.

Let go of the internal chant and sit in silent contemplation of yourself as a creature of earth – solid, heavy, cold, and dry.

Pause for a couple of breaths.

Take note of the emotions, pleasant and unpleasant, that you associate with the qualities of earth, as well as the vices and virtues that seem most fitting for this element.

Pause for several breaths.

Now, within your body of stone, move your attention to your lower abdomen, a place corresponding to the element of water. In a moment, we will begin chanting the vowel sound OO and, as we do so, imagine yourself becoming even more a creature of water, your stony body getting wetter and wetter, making you feel more fluid. Yet these changes are comfortable and welcome, as you desire to more fully experience the special energies of water. We are about to begin the chant.

Begin the chant ooooooo and continue through at least five repetitions.

Rest and continue the chant silently within, while seeing and feeling your body dissolving into a living puddle of water – translucent, cool, and still.

Pause for a few breaths.

Let go of the internal chant and sit in silent contemplation of yourself as a creature of water – fluid, cool, and still.

Pause for a couple of breaths.

Take note of the emotions, pleasant and unpleasant, that you associate with the qualities of water, as well as the vices and virtues that seem most fitting for this element.

Pause for several breaths.

Now, within your body of water, move your attention to your solar plexus, a place corresponding to the element of fire. In a moment, we will begin chanting the vowel sound OH and, as we do so, imagine yourself becoming even more a creature of fire, getting drier and drier, hotter and hotter, making you feel lighter, more and more active. Yet these changes are comfortable and welcome, as you desire to more fully experience the special energies of fire. We are about to begin the chant.

Begin the chant oooohhhh and continue through at least five repetitions.

Rest and continue the chant silently within, while seeing and feeling your body transforming into one of living flames – hot, dry, and flickering brightly.

Pause for a few breaths.

Let go of the internal chant and sit in silent contemplation of yourself as a creature of fire – flaming, bright, hot, and dry.

Pause for a couple of breaths.

Take note of the emotions, pleasant and unpleasant, that you associate with the qualities of fire, as well as the vices and virtues that seem most fitting for this element.

Pause for several breaths.

Now, within your body of fire, move your attention to your chest, a place corresponding to the element of air. In a moment, we will begin chanting the vowel sound AH and, as we do so, imagine yourself becoming even more a creature of air, getting less and less substantial, your flames cooling a bit and becoming thinner and thinner, making you feel lighter and lighter, more and more vaporous. Yet these changes are comfortable and welcome, as you desire to more fully experience the special energies of air. We are about to begin the chant.

Begin the chant aaaahhhh and continue through at least five repetitions.

Rest and continue the chant silently within, while seeing and feeling your body evaporating into a living atmosphere of warm, dry air.

Pause for a few breaths.

Let go of the internal chant and sit in silent contemplation of yourself as a creature of air – floating, warm, and dry.

Pause for a couple of breaths.

Take note of the emotions, pleasant and unpleasant, that you associate with the qualities of air, as well as the vices and virtues that seem most fitting for this element.

Pause for several breaths.

Now, within your body of air, move your attention to your throat, a place corresponding to the element of aether. In a moment, we will begin chanting the vowel sound I and, as we do so, sense yourself becoming more a spirit of the mysterious aether, becoming quieter and quieter, less and less substantial, less and less definable in terms of space and time. Yet these changes are comfortable and welcome, as you desire to more fully experience the special energies of aether. We are about to begin the chant.

Begin the chant iiiiiiiiiiiiiii and continue through at least five repetitions.

Rest and continue the chant silently within, while sensing yourself disappearing into mysterious, timeless, boundless spirit.

Pause for a few breaths.

Let go of the internal chant and sit in silent contemplation of spirit.

Pause for several breaths.

Now, within the mysterious spirit, feel your body beginning to re-form with thin breezes of air, growing warm with the emergence of flames as if in a cloud of gas, thickening and becoming more fluid with the condensing of water, and finally solidifying into human flesh and bones with the formation of earth.

Pause for a couple of breaths.

You are now aware of all the elements in your body: the earthiness of your flesh and bones; the wateriness of all your fluids; the fieriness of your electromagnetic field and heat generating processes; the airi-ness of your respiration and the oxygenation of all your cells; and the aetheric mystery of your spirit. For a moment sit in awareness of your whole being as a harmonious integration of these elements.

Pause for several breaths.

RECONNECT WITH THE PRESENT AND END THE MEDITATION

Release the imagery and again clear your mind as you attend to the sensations of your body right here. Feel gravity pulling you down into your seat and your feet against the floor. Feel the air on your skin and your breath flowing in and out. Hear what you hear. Smell what you smell and taste what you taste. When you are ready, open your eyes and see what you see.

The meditation has ended. Feel free to move and stretch your limbs.

REFLECTION

Invite participants to share their experiences, insights, and questions. Remember to use these skills:

- *welcoming sharing*

- *active listening*

- *scanning the group*

- *managing the flow*

- *being careful with advice*

WRAP UP AND CLOSE

Announce that it is time to end the session. Restate some of the more common or poignant reflections. Inform participants about the next time and location for meditation or other contemplative activities. Thank everyone for their participation.

APPENDIX D:
PRE- AND POST-RITUAL SCRIPTS

*THESE SCRIPTS ARE SUITABLE FOR USE
IN CONJUNCTION WITH CEREMONIES OF INITIATION
INTO ANY DEGREE OR INSTALLATION INTO ANY OFFICE.*

SCRIPT #1: PRE-RITUAL FOR CANDIDATES

Become thoroughly familiar with this script before using it to facilitate an activity. Notes and additional guidelines for the facilitator appear in italics, and spoken parts are indicated by a regular font. Consider your audience and what, if any, adjustments you might make in facilitating this activity. Ensure that the space is appropriately prepared. <u>Note that all members are welcome to participate in this meditation in addition to candidates.</u>

WELCOME PARTICIPANTS

Thank everyone for coming and state it is time to focus on meditation. <u>Remind others to be mindful of what they say so as not to reveal any of the secrets of the upcoming degree to candidates.</u> Ask for cell phones to be completely silenced and set an example by letting others see you doing so. Ask if you are speaking loudly enough for everyone to clearly hear you.

PROVIDE INTRODUCTIONS AS NEEDED

Unless you are certain everyone knows you, tell them your name, your connection with the fraternity, and that you will be facilitating the meditation for this session. Consider whether or not it would be helpful and time-efficient to welcome participants to introduce themselves.

EXPLAIN WHAT TO EXPECT

In this session, I am following a script from *The Contemplative Lodge: A Manual for Masons Doing Inner Work Together.* We will contemplate the coming ceremony, our places in it, and things that have brought us to its advent. Are there any questions?

RELAXATION AND CENTERING

Closing your eyes or gazing blankly at some point in front of you, begin to relax and turn your attention inward. If you wish, take a moment to silently invoke the aid of Deity.

Pause for several breaths.

Slowly take in a deep breath, inhaling all the air you can without straining, and then hold it, hold it, hold it. Now release the breath, exhaling all the air you can without straining, and then pause, pause, pause.

Slowly take in a second deep breath, inhaling all the air you can without straining, and then hold it, hold it, hold it. Now release the breath, exhaling all the air you can without straining, and then pause, pause, pause.

Slowly take in a third deep breath, inhaling all the air you can without straining, and then hold it, hold it, hold it. Now release the breath, exhaling all the air you can without straining, and then pause, pause, pause. Now inhale and let your body breathe in its own peaceful, natural rhythm.

Pause for a couple of breaths.

Attend to the sensation of the earth's gravity pulling down on your body. Feel it pulling your feet against the floor. Feel gravity pulling down in your calves and shins. If you notice any unnecessary tension in those muscles, let it go, and let the pull of gravity take you into a deeper state of calm, peaceful relaxation.

Pause for a couple of breaths.

Feel gravity pulling down in your thighs and buttocks, pulling you into your seat. If you notice any unnecessary tension in those muscles, let it go, and let the pull of gravity take you into a deeper state of calm, peaceful relaxation.

Pause for a couple of breaths.

Feel gravity pulling down in your hips, belly, and lower back. If you notice any unnecessary tension in those muscles, let it go, leaving only what is necessary to keep you sitting in a healthy posture, and let the pull of gravity take you into a deeper state of calm, peaceful relaxation.

Pause for a couple of breaths.

Feel gravity pulling down in your ribcage, chest, and upper back. If you notice any unnecessary tension in those muscles, let it go, leaving only what is necessary to keep you sitting in a healthy posture, and let the pull of gravity take you into a deeper state of calm, peaceful relaxation.

Pause for a couple of breaths.

Feel gravity pulling down in your shoulders and neck. If you notice any unnecessary tension in those muscles, let it go, leaving only what is necessary to keep you sitting in a healthy posture, and let the pull of gravity take you into a deeper state of calm, peaceful relaxation.

Pause for a couple of breaths.

Feel gravity pulling down in your upper arms, forearms, wrists, and hands. If you notice any unnecessary tension in those muscles, let it go, and let the pull of gravity take you into a deeper state of calm, peaceful relaxation.

Pause for a couple of breaths.

Feel gravity pulling down in your jaw, your tongue, around your mouth, and in your cheeks. Feel gravity pulling down around your eyes and in your brow. Feel gravity pulling down in your scalp on the top of your head, around the sides, and down the back. If you notice any unnecessary tension in those muscles, let it go, leaving only what is necessary to keep you sitting in a healthy posture, and let the pull of gravity take you into a deeper state of calm, peaceful relaxation.

Pause for a couple of breaths.

Now, feel gravity pulling down from the top of your head all the way through every part of your body down to the soles of your feet. If you notice any unnecessary tension anywhere, let it go, leaving only what

is necessary to keep you sitting in a healthy posture, and let the pull of gravity take you into a deeper state of calm, peaceful relaxation.

Pause for a couple of breaths.

Turn your attention back to your breath, flowing in and out in its own peaceful, natural rhythm. Simply observe it flowing in and out in its own peaceful, natural rhythm. Feel each breath taking you into a deeper state of calm, peaceful relaxation.

Pause for a few breaths.

You can go into an even deeper state of calm, peaceful relaxation by silently marking the breath with the word "in" as you inhale, and "out" as you exhale: iiiiiinnn, ooouuut. Just continue observing the breath flowing in and out in its own peaceful, natural rhythm as you continue silently repeating: iiiiiinnn, ooouuut. Feel each breath taking you into a deeper state of calm, peaceful relaxation.

Pause for several breaths.

PRE-RITUAL PROCESS

Realize that you are now on the threshold of significant event. It is an event of enacting and celebrating a transition of movement from what was into what will be – an ending and a beginning.

Pause for a couple of breaths.

Many things of the past have led you to this moment and the role you will play in the coming ceremony.

Pause for a couple of breaths.

Why are you going through the coming ceremony? What is your purpose?

Pause for a few breaths.

What desires have led you?

Pause for a few breaths.

What do you hope will result from the coming ceremony?

Pause for a few breaths.

How did those desires and hopes arise in you? Where did they come from?

Pause for a few breaths.

What considerations and decisions have you made to get this far?

Pause for a few breaths.

What actions have you taken to get this far? What sacrifices have you made?

Pause for a few breaths.

Looking far back into your past, what can you see that has led you to believe it is important for you to go through the coming ceremony?

Pause for a few breaths.

What similar experiences have you had, and how is this one similar yet also different?

Pause for a few breaths.

What emotions do you feel as you ponder this moment and the coming ceremony?

Pause for a few breaths.

What do those feelings tell you about this event, your place in it, and yourself?

Pause for a few breaths.

Other than yourself, who or what has been most helpful to you coming to this moment?

Pause for a few breaths.

What, if anything, do you feel you owe for the help you have already received?

Pause for a few breaths.

How do you intend to conduct yourself in the coming ceremony?

Pause for a few breaths.

What attitudes and emotions are most fitting for your role?

Pause for a few breaths.

You will hear all these questions once more, and then you will have time to silently contemplate them for a while. You may find that some demand your attention more than others, and you are encouraged to trust yourself in that regard.

- Why are you going through the coming ceremony? What is your purpose?

- What desires have led you this far?

- What do you hope will result from the coming ceremony?

- How did those desires and hopes arise in you? Where did they come from?

- What considerations and decisions have you made to get this far?

- What actions have you taken to get this far? What sacrifices have you made?

- Looking far back into your past, what can you see that has led you to believe it is important for you to go through this ceremony?

- What similar experiences have you had, and how is this one similar yet also different?

- What emotions do you feel as you ponder this moment and the coming ceremony?

- What do those feelings tell you about this event, your place in it, and yourself?

- Other than yourself, who or what has been most helpful to you coming to this moment?

- What, if anything, do you feel you owe for the help you have already received?

- How do you intend to conduct yourself in the coming ceremony?

- What attitudes and emotions are most fitting for your role?

Pause for at least a few minutes.

Let go of the questions for now and take a moment to prepare yourself to be mindfully present in the ceremony, fully attending to it and receptive to its effects.

Pause for a few breaths.

RECONNECT WITH THE PRESENT AND END THE MEDITATION

Now clear your mind as you attend to the sensations of your body right here. Feel gravity pulling you down into your seat and your feet against the floor. Feel the air on your skin and your breath flowing in and out. Hear what you hear. Smell what you smell and taste what you taste. When you are ready open your eyes and see what you see.

The meditation has ended. Feel free to move and stretch your limbs.

REFLECTION

Remind members to be mindful of what participants say so as not to reveal any of the secrets of the coming degree to candidates. Invite everybody to share their experiences, insights, and questions. *Be prepared to review the questions asked during the meditation.* Remember to use these skills:

- *welcoming sharing*
- *active listening*
- *scanning the group*
- *managing the flow*
- *being careful with advice*

WRAP UP AND CLOSE

Announce that it is time to end the session. Restate some of the more common or poignant reflections. Inform participants about the next time and location for meditation or other contemplative activities. Thank everyone for their participation.

SCRIPT #2: PRE-RITUAL FOR CEREMONIAL TEAM AND OBSERVERS

Become thoroughly familiar with this script before using it to facilitate an activity. Notes and additional guidelines for the facilitator appear in italics, and spoken parts are indicated by a regular font. Consider your audience and what, if any, adjustments you might make in facilitating this activity. Ensure that the space is appropriately prepared.

WELCOME PARTICIPANTS

Thank everyone for coming and state it is time to focus on meditation. Ensure that no degree candidates are present. Ask for cell phones to be completely silenced and set an example by letting others see you doing so. Ask if you are speaking loudly enough for everyone to clearly hear you.

PROVIDE INTRODUCTIONS AS NEEDED

Unless you are certain everyone knows you, tell them your name, your connection with the fraternity, and that you will be facilitating the meditation for this session. Consider whether or not it would be helpful and time-efficient to welcome participants to introduce themselves.

EXPLAIN WHAT TO EXPECT

In this session, I am following a script from *The Contemplative Lodge: A Manual for Masons Doing Inner Work Together*. We will contemplate the coming ceremony, our places in it, and how we may best contribute to its effectiveness. Are there any questions?

RELAXATION AND CENTERING

Closing your eyes or gazing blankly at some point in front of you, begin to relax and turn your attention inward. If you wish, take a moment to silently invoke the aid of Deity.

Pause for several breaths.

Slowly take in a deep breath, inhaling all the air you can without straining, and then hold it, hold it, hold it. Now release the breath, exhaling all the air you can without straining, and then pause, pause, pause.

Slowly take in a second deep breath, inhaling all the air you can without straining, and then hold it, hold it, hold it. Now release the breath, exhaling all the air you can without straining, and then pause, pause, pause.

Slowly take in a third deep breath, inhaling all the air you can without straining, and then hold it, hold it, hold it. Now release the breath, exhaling all the air you can without straining, and then pause, pause, pause. Now inhale and let your body breathe in its own peaceful, natural rhythm.

Pause for a couple of breaths.

Attend to the sensation of the earth's gravity pulling down on your body. Feel it pulling your feet against the floor. Feel gravity pulling down in your calves and shins. If you notice any unnecessary tension in those muscles, let it go, and let the pull of gravity take you into a deeper state of calm, peaceful relaxation.

Pause for a couple of breaths.

Feel gravity pulling down in your thighs and buttocks, pulling you into your seat. If you notice any unnecessary tension in those muscles, let it go, and let the pull of gravity take you into a deeper state of calm, peaceful relaxation.

Pause for a couple of breaths.

Feel gravity pulling down in your hips, belly, and lower back. If you notice any unnecessary tension in those muscles, let it go, leaving only what is necessary to keep you sitting in a healthy posture, and let the pull of gravity take you into a deeper state of calm, peaceful relaxation.

Pause for a couple of breaths.

Feel gravity pulling down in your ribcage, chest, and upper back. If you notice any unnecessary tension in those muscles, let it go, leaving only what is necessary to keep you sitting in a healthy posture, and let the pull of gravity take you into a deeper state of calm, peaceful relaxation.

Pause for a couple of breaths.

Feel gravity pulling down in your shoulders and neck. If you notice any unnecessary tension in those muscles, let it go, leaving only what is necessary to keep you sitting in a healthy posture, and let the pull of gravity take you into a deeper state of calm, peaceful relaxation.

Pause for a couple of breaths.

Feel gravity pulling down in your upper arms, forearms, wrists, and hands. If you notice any unnecessary tension in those muscles, let it go, and let the pull of gravity take you into a deeper state of calm, peaceful relaxation.

Pause for a couple of breaths.

Feel gravity pulling down in your jaw, your tongue, around your mouth, and in your cheeks. Feel gravity pulling down around your eyes and in your brow. Feel gravity pulling down in your scalp on the top of your head, around the sides, and down the back. If you notice any unnecessary tension in those muscles, let it go, leaving only what is necessary to keep you sitting in a healthy posture, and let the pull of gravity take you into a deeper state of calm, peaceful relaxation.

Pause for a couple of breaths.

Now, feel gravity pulling down from the top of your head all the way through every part of your body down to the soles of your feet. If you notice any unnecessary tension anywhere, let it go, leaving only what

is necessary to keep you sitting in a healthy posture, and let the pull of gravity take you into a deeper state of calm, peaceful relaxation.

Pause for a couple of breaths.

Turn your attention back to your breath, flowing in and out in its own peaceful, natural rhythm. Simply observe it flowing in and out in its own peaceful, natural rhythm. Feel each breath taking you into a deeper state of calm, peaceful relaxation.

Pause for a few breaths.

You can go into an even deeper state of calm, peaceful relaxation by silently marking the breath with the word "in" as you inhale, and "out" as you exhale: iiiiiinnn, ooouuut. Just continue observing the breath flowing in and out in its own peaceful, natural rhythm as you continue silently repeating: iiiiiinnn, ooouuut. Feel each breath taking you into a deeper state of calm, peaceful relaxation.

Pause for several breaths.

PRE-RITUAL PROCESS

Why do you want to be in the coming ceremony?

Pause for a few breaths.

Why might it be important to others that you are there?

Pause for a few breaths.

What is your role, and what are its functions in the ceremony?

Pause for a few breaths.

What symbols are associated with your role, such as a mythic character, a jewel, or an apron? Remember that even as an observer, you still at least wear the apron of your highest degree.

Pause for a few breaths.

What virtues, attitudes, emotions, and subtle energies are evoked by those symbols for you?

Pause for several breaths.

What if any other psychological, philosophical, or spiritual significance do you associate with your role?

Pause for a few breaths.

Now imagine yourself actually connecting with the symbols of your role. Mentally put on your apron and put on your jewel if your role has one. As you put them on, feel the qualities and energies they represent becoming amplified in your body, mind, and soul.

Pause for several breaths.

If your role is associated with a specific character, then allow yourself to identify with that character, feeling the qualities and attitudes associated with that character becoming more amplified in your body, mind, and soul.

Pause for several breaths.

Imagine yourself performing your role during the ceremony, mindful of your functions and projecting its qualities, attitudes, and energies through your presence and actions.

Pause for several breaths.

Imagine experiencing others performing their roles as effective representatives of the corresponding qualities, attitudes, and energies.

Pause for several breaths.

What visualizations might assist you in appropriately projecting your qualities, attitudes, and energies as well as experiencing those of others during the ceremony? Imagine yourself using them.

Pause for several breaths.

Now imagine yourself removing your apron, as well as your jewel if you wore one. Feel yourself releasing your identification with your role and any mythic character associated with it. Affirm to yourself that you have returned to your actual personality and that you can reassume the qualities, attitudes, and energies of your role when the time comes.

Pause for several breaths.

Reconnect with the Present and End the Meditation

Now clear your mind as you attend to the sensations of your body right here. Feel gravity pulling you down into your seat and your feet against the floor. Feel the air on your skin and your breath flowing in and out. Hear what you hear. Smell what you smell and taste what you taste. When you are ready open your eyes and see what you see.

The meditation has ended. Feel free to move and stretch your limbs.

REFLECTION

Invite participants to share their experiences, insights, and questions. Be prepared to review the questions and instructions presented during the meditation. Remember to use these skills:

- *welcoming sharing*
- *active listening*
- *scanning the group*
- *managing the flow*
- *being careful with advice*

WRAP UP AND CLOSE

Announce that it is time to end the session. Restate some of the more common or poignant reflections. Inform participants about the next time and location for meditation or other contemplative activities. Thank everyone for their participation.

SCRIPT #3: POST-RITUAL FOR ALL

Become thoroughly familiar with this script before using it to facilitate an activity. Notes and additional guidelines for the facilitator appear in italics, and spoken parts are indicated by a regular font. Consider your audience and what, if any, adjustments you might make in facilitating this activity. Ensure that the space is appropriately prepared.

WELCOME PARTICIPANTS

Thank everyone for coming and state that it is time to focus on contemplative discourse. Ask for cell phones to be completely silenced and set an example by letting others see you doing so. Ask if you are speaking loudly enough for everyone to clearly hear you.

PROVIDE INTRODUCTIONS AS NEEDED

Unless you are certain everyone knows you, tell them your name, your connection with the fraternity, and that you will be facilitating the contemplative discourse. Consider whether or not it would be helpful and time-efficient to welcome participants to introduce themselves.

Explain What to Expect

In this session, I am following a script from *The Contemplative Lodge: A Manual for Masons Doing Inner Work Together*. We will have discourse on the recent ceremony of _____, making use of the W^3 technique. The basis of this technique is remembering and addressing three simple questions:

- *"What?"* – This question is about the simple facts of the ritual and the most basic observations made as they were happening.

- *"So what?"* – Attention is given to analyzing, speculating, and conceptualizing about lessons, meanings, and uses for what was learned.

- *"Now what?"* – The focus becomes when, where, and how any conclusions will be applied and tested.

As we explore possibilities, we affirm that no individual or organization within the Craft has the right to demand that Masons limit their personal understandings to the traditional meanings, just as individuals should not expect their personal meanings be approved or adopted by others. While an openness to different perspectives and understandings is vital to contemplative discourse, so is the effort to carefully examine things, clarify our thinking about them, and consider their usefulness for improving our lives or the lives of others. Are there any questions?

Relaxation and Centering

Closing your eyes or gazing blankly at some point in front of you, begin to relax and turn your attention inward. If you wish, take a moment to silently invoke the aid of Deity.

Pause for several breaths.

Slowly take in a deep breath, inhaling all the air you can without straining, and then hold it, hold it, hold it. Now release the breath, exhaling all the air you can without straining, and then pause, pause, pause.

Slowly take in a second deep breath, inhaling all the air you can without straining, and then hold it, hold it, hold it. Now release the breath, exhaling all the air you can without straining, and then pause, pause, pause.

Slowly take in a third deep breath, inhaling all the air you can without straining, and then hold it, hold it, hold it. Now release the breath, exhaling all the air you can without straining, and then pause, pause, pause. Now inhale and let your body breathe in its own peaceful, natural rhythm.

Pause for a few breaths.

Focal Point

Our focal point for this session is the recent ceremony of
_____. Concentrate on your memories of the event,
making it the central point within the circle of your thoughts and
feelings. If you participated in a pre-ritual meditation, recall its relevance to the actual experience.

Pause for several breaths.

Discourse

Now open your eyes and bring your attention back to the group so
that we may begin our discourse.

*For the allotted time, invite participants to share their experiences, in-
sights, and questions. Remember to use these skills:*

- *welcoming sharing*
- *active listening*
- *scanning the group*
- *managing the flow*
- *being careful with advice*

Consider using the following questions to prompt sharing.

What?

- *What were the emblems, furniture, regalia, and
  other things that got your attention?*

- *What else did you see, hear, smell, or taste?*

- *What roles or parts were played in the ritual?*

- *What were its events?*

- *What patterns did you observe?*

- *What do you recall thinking or feeling at different points along the way?*

- *What are your general feelings about it now?*

So what?

- *What were the ritual's purposes, its motives, and intentions?*

- *What were your motives and intentions?*

- *Why are those motives and intentions important?*

- *In what ways does this experience connect with other experiences you have had or things you know?*

- *What seemed to be the most obvious lessons?*

- *What other possibilities of meaning might there be?*

- *What questions has this experience raised in your mind?*

- *How might these lessons and questions be personally relevant and useful to you?*

Now what?

- *What can you do to productively respond to your questions?*

- *How might you act on the lessons of the ritual?*

- *In what specific ways might you experiment with changing your thoughts and actions?*

- *What are some specific times and places you can enact and test these changes in the near future?*

- *During and after your attempts to use what you learned, who will you discuss them with?*

WRAP UP AND CLOSE

Announce that it is time to end the session. Ask participants to spend a moment in silent reflection on the discourse. After pausing for several breaths, restate some of the more common or poignant reflections and speculations. Inform participants about the next time and location for contemplative discourse or other contemplative activities. Thank everyone for their participation.

INDEX

ABOUT THE AUTHOR

Chuck Dunning has over three decades of experience as a practitioner, advocate, consultant, and facilitator of contemplation. In his career in higher education and mental health, in Masonry, and with other groups and individuals, he facilitates and teaches mindfulness, meditation, and imagery to enhance peoples' experiences of life in many ways.

Contemplative Masonry: Basic Applications of Mindfulness, Meditation, and Imagery for the Craft, was Chuck's first book, published in 2016. In 2018, the readers of *Fraternal Review*, the magazine of the Southern California Research Lodge, recognized him as among the top 10 authors in Masonic esotericism. In 2019, he received the Thomas W. Jackson Masonic Education Award at the College of Freemasonry in Rochester, New York. He is also a contributing author in *The Art & Science of Initiation*, published by Lewis Masonic in 2019.

Chuck has been a Master Mason since 1988, and he is a Full Member of the Texas Lodge of Research. In the Scottish Rite, Chuck is a Knight Commander of the Court of Honor, Director of Education for the Guthrie Valley in Oklahoma, and a Class Director for the Fort Worth Valley in Texas. In 2012, he became the founding Superintendent of the Academy of Reflection, a chartered organization for Scottish Rite Masons wanting to integrate contemplative practice with their Masonic experience.

To learn more about Chuck's work in contemplative practice, visit his website at www.chuckdunning.com. For inquiries about his services as a contemplative advocate, consultant, or facilitator, please send email to:

chuck@chuckdunning.com

www.ingramcontent.com/pod-product-compliance
Lightning Source LLC
LaVergne TN
LVHW051455080426
835509LV00017B/1770